Barcode in Back

MW01121460

WHILE WE'RE YOUNG

WHILE WE'RE YOUNG

by Don Hannah

Playwrights Canada Press
Toronto • Canada

While We're Young © 2009 Don Hannah
Introduction © 2009 Kim McCaw
PLAYWRIGHTS CANADA PRESS
The Canadian Drama Publisher
215 Spadina Ave., Suite 230, Toronto, Ontario, Canada M5T 2C7
phone 416.703.0013   fax 416.408.3402
orders@playwrightscanada.com • www.playwrightscanada.com

For professional or amateur production rights, please contact
Kensington Literary Representation, 34 St. Andrew Street, Toronto, Ontario,
Canada M5T 1K6, 416.979.0187, kensingtonlit@rogers.com

The publisher acknowledges the support of the Canadian taxpayers through the
Government of Canada Book Publishing Industry Development Program, the
Canada Council for the Arts, the Ontario Arts Council, and the Ontario Media
Development Corporation.

Production editor: Michael Petrasek
Cover design: Micheline Courtemanche

LIBRARY AND ARCHIVES CANADA CATALOGUING IN PUBLICATION

Hannah, Don, 1951-
While we're young / Don Hannah

A play.
ISBN 978-0-88754-877-2

I. Title.

PS8565.A583W45 2009   C812'.54   C2009-904746-2

First edition: November 2009
Printed and bound in Canada by Canadian Printco, Scarborough

For Dayne Ogilvie
1950–2006

Introduction

Don Hannah came to the University of Alberta in the fall of 2006 as the inaugural Lee Playwright-in-Residence. This position, the first of its kind in Canadian universities, is made possible through a legacy endowment from the Clifford E. Lee Foundation. The program funds a professional playwright to spend two years at the university, doing their own work and acting as a resource to students and the broader theatre community.

The residency also includes a commission to write a new play for a graduating BFA acting class that will be presented in the department's Studio Theatre season. It is an opportunity to create an original work, customized to a particular acting class, taking advantage of various special qualities they may have. It also addresses a real challenge that faces many theatre-training programs—finding plays that provide a range of meaningful roles for large casts (usually around twelve each year).

The commission can be seen as something of a mixed blessing. On the one hand, it's money in a playwright's hands and a virtual commitment of production, which isn't easily obtained elsewhere. On the other hand, the task is a difficult one: write a play for production in two years that will provide meaningful roles for twelve student actors. In developing our plans for the residency, we had discussions with other playwrights about commissions of this nature and received widely varied responses: one playwright was adamant that he would never accept such an assignment because it would mean two years of sweating over a play that would have such a large cast that it would never be produced again. Others were very keen to take on the artistic challenge. Happily, Don fell in the latter category, and it was through this commission that Don wrote the beautiful *While We're Young*.

When the Department of Drama created the playwright-in-residence position, Don was one of the very first people I thought of to fill the role. I have known Don for quite some time. Our paths first crossed years ago at the Banff Playwrights Colony while I was working as John Murrell's associate. I had known Don's work from his long association with Toronto's Tarragon Theatre, but was truly knocked out by the play he brought to Banff on this occasion, *Running Far Back*. That script packed an emotional punch that isn't matched very often. His aching portrait of a troubled Maritime family moved me deeply. I felt it was one of the finest pieces of theatrical writing I had encountered and am baffled by the fact that it is so rarely produced by Canadian theatres. Almost by chance, I ran into him at the Magnetic North Theatre Festival in Ottawa and took the opportunity to tell him about the residency, strongly encouraging him to put his name forward. He sighed, and said something like, "But I'm in a relationship!" I took that to mean there was little chance we'd be able to lure him out to wintery Edmonton for two years, but was surprised and delighted when his letter arrived, letting us know of his keen interest in the post. Our selection committee was universal in its enthusiasm for Don as our inaugural playwright, and he certainly lived up to all of our hopes and expectations. (I am very happy and more than a little relieved to know that the relationship still thrives despite the many months of separation imposed on it by Don's time spent with us.)

Don was a wonderful choice as the first Lee Playwright-in-Residence. The first and most important reason is simply his talent as a writer. He creates stories with deep emotional roots and complex, achingly human characters who speak in a language that mixes the sound of the everyday with a hint of the poetic, lifting them into theatrical reality. He is also an articulate, caring, generous dramaturge, who can always find a valuable comment for any writer bringing new material to him for response. Don was great with students, emerging writers, and, on occasion, with the more seasoned professionals in the Edmonton community. He had an open door and an open heart for anyone who wanted feedback.

While We're Young was a joy to work on in rehearsal. Don was present virtually every day, which isn't always what one wants from a playwright, but in this case was ideal. As the director, I felt complete support and trust from him throughout, and his gentle presence and insightful comments along the way were invaluable. Because his writing process is so meticulous and careful, there was very little in the way of editing or rewriting during rehearsals. Some small cuts were made to sharpen the focus of a few scenes and dialogue was fine-tuned, but the structure, character, story, and themes were always there and remained strong and true all the way to opening night.

I am truly impressed with how he went about creating this fabulous, complex play. In a stroke of wisdom (and genius, perhaps), he made the decision to use the fact that the whole cast would be in their early twenties as an opportunity rather than an obstacle. What we got was a play in which everyone played characters their own age, with similar life experiences (albeit in different historical eras) and similar life challenges (falling in love, dealing with parental pressures, imagining what the future might hold for them). Don spent a lot of time with the class who would be performing the show, and their individual and collective personalities informed and inspired his writing.

He made a crucial decision fairly early in the writing process not to create characters for specific actors in the class, but to develop a collection of characters that provided roles for everyone (it became eleven people after one student left the program at the end of the first year) and could be played by any number of different actors from the class. As we began our workshop and development process with the play, we decided to keep working in this way. That meant that each time we had a new reading of the evolving script, we deliberately shuffled the casting around. After a number of different sessions, we had managed to hear virtually every person in the class read every possible combination of roles. One of the real benefits of this approach was that while the class as a whole gained a wonderful sense of ownership of the play, no one was able to invest too heavily in any particular character or part. To be honest, it did become clear early on that a couple of roles had some special attraction, and a couple of the students made it clear where their hearts lay in the casting sweepstakes. But, in the end, Don had created a marvel: a profoundly moving play with eleven fabulous roles for young actors. It's a piece that should become an eternally popular choice for theatre programs across North America. Not to mention becoming a feature on professional stages as well.

Almost two years later, I'm still struck by the interesting contradictions in the play. On the one hand, it has an air of freshness and immediacy with its storyline about the young people in Edmonton and the impact of the ongoing Afghan conflict on their lives. On the other, it travels comfortably through Canadian geography and history, taking us to Toronto in the thirties and forties, to the battlefields of Flanders, to rural Nova Scotia decades ago. It is a very big story constructed from a lot of little stories—half a dozen plot lines woven together to create one family saga, an historical epic told in a series of small, intimate, immensely actable scenes. It's a war story, a number of love stories (both happy and tragic), a comedy, a drama, and a poetic gem. It has soldiers and singers, lovers and losers, friends and enemies. It loudly and proudly celebrates its Canadian heart and soul. We see how things are different and yet the same, we see how some values are eternal, while others are shaped by familial and societal pressures that evolve and change. We see the overwhelming power of family over us all. We see how individual choices reverberate through generations, and how the sins of our ancestors affect us today. And, in the end, we see how the power of love is what makes us truly human and keeps us going together forever.

Kim McCaw
Professor and Associate Chair
Department of Drama
University of Alberta

Playwright's Note

While We're Young was written for a talented class of acting students at the University of Alberta's drama department. I was the Lee Playwright-in-Residence there from January 2006 to May 2007, and the play opened early in 2008, their graduating year. When I first arrived in Edmonton, I knew only two things about the proposed play: that it should be an ensemble piece with good parts for all, and that I wanted the characters to be the same age as the actors. The story, the structure—everything else—evolved from there.

We were smart enough to have the actors read *While We're Young* at various stages of its development; each time Kim McCaw and I recast so that no actor read the same role twice. This meant that I heard a variety of voices for each character, and it also meant that the actors grew to have a sense of ownership, not of individual parts but of the piece as a whole. They knew that this play belonged to them. In the past, playwrights wrote for acting companies; writing *While We're Young* made me wish that this were still and always the case. In the best of all possible worlds, every playwright could be writing for a company as talented and committed as mine. (As you can see, I grew to have a sense of ownership, too.) Working on *While We're Young* became the happiest playwriting experience I'd had in a very long while.

I want especially to acknowledge one person, my great friend Dayne Ogilvie. Like Mac and Paul in the play, Dayne and I went way back—in our case, to the sixties, to King George School in Moncton, N.B. We hung out together in Toronto for over twenty-five years. While he was the editor of *Xtra*, he gave me work as a reviewer, and he and his partner Gary Akenhead generously loaned me their little house in Nova Scotia as a place I could go and write. No one has encouraged and supported me more.

Dayne left Moncton in the late sixties and came to study acting at the U of A; he had fallen in love with Tennessee Williams and Samuel Beckett, and that's where they led him. More than three decades later, I was playwright-in-residence in his old department. At the end of my first year in Edmonton, he came back to visit me. We had a lovely celebratory dinner—our birthdays being close together—and then walked about in Garneau because he wanted to show me a house where he had lived when he was young. When he couldn't find it, he became quite silly—ditsy queens were a specialty of his—and we laughed about growing middle-aged and forgetful. Finally he shrugged and had to admit that the house of his student days was probably gone.

Four months later, suddenly, terribly, out of the blue, he was gone as well. With Dayne's death, I felt so far away from my life back east, from my partner and friends. What sustained me was this project, and the talent and commitment of this company. This play, which jumps about in time and is set in a world filled with generations of young people, is for my friend who was, when he was young, a member of a company much like the one I was lucky enough to call mine. I cherish that connection.

Production Notes

The set should be as simple as possible to allow for swift and elegant transitions from scene to scene and from one time period to another. The production needs to focus on costumes and lighting.

In the second act, during the two final scenes, "The Darkening Landscape" and "The Sunny Day," the set needs to be able to transform into large dramatic pictures. As these two scenes evolve, and the various stories and generations come and go, the effect might resemble a painting by Poussin: a landscape populated by various individuals and groups—not a naturalistic landscape, of course, but an emotional one.

Costumes should root the play in time and place, but they should not editorialize, and they should be mindful of the characters' social and economic backgrounds. For example, for the characters in this play, Pictou County in the nineteenth century was a hardscrabble existence: farmers were poor and ministers were very badly paid.

While We're Young opened at the Timms Centre for the Arts, Edmonton, in February 2008 in a production directed by Kim McCaw. The set was designed by Guido Tondino, Robert Shannon did the costumes, and Lee Livingstone the lights. Oscar Guzman was the sound designer, Michele Brown was vocal coach, and Linda Rubin the movement coach. The stage managers were Anna Wood and Allie Bailey. The cast as follows:

DYLAN/ROSS	Richard Lee
CLAIRE	Stacy Berg
PETER/CLARENCE	Garett Spelliscy
DEBBI/MAUDE	Ava Jane Markus
RANDY/MAC	Scott Shpeley
JOANNE	Jennifer Fader
HELEN/OLD DORA	Elena Porter
DOLLY/ CLARA	Jenny McKillop
PAUL/IVAN	Ryan Parker
JAMIE	Cole Humney
DORA	Kirsten Rasmussen
YOUNG JAMIE	Adam MacMahon

There were readings at Vancouver's Playwrights Theatre Centre, the Banff Playwrights Colony, and the National Theatre School, many thanks to all concerned.

My love to Doug, for his support and understanding through two long winters.

Characters

With one exception, all of the characters in *While We're Young* are between the ages of eighteen and twenty-five. The exception is YOUNG JAMIE, who is a young boy of five or six. In chronological order, they are:

> 1870s Nova Scotia
> > CLARA
> > CLARENCE
> > MAUDE
> > OLD DORA (a ghost)
>
> 1890s and turn-of-the-century Nova Scotia
> > DORA
> > ROSS
> > YOUNG JAMIE
>
> First World War Flanders
> > MAC
> > JAMIE
> > PAUL
>
> Late 1930s, early 1940s, Toronto and Edmonton
> > DOLLY
> > HELEN
> > IVAN
>
> Early 1970s Edmonton
> > JOANNE
> > RANDY
> > DEBBI
>
> 2007–2008 Edmonton
> > DYLAN
> > CLAIRE
> > PETER

In addition, there are NEIGHBOURS (1870), SOLDIERS (1917), a CHURCH CHOIR (1899), and MUSICIANS (1939).

The play was originally written for a cast of twelve that broke down in this way: one child, five men, six women.

ACT ONE

Scene 1: 2006

Edmonton, a warm evening in summer.

CLAIRE and DYLAN are drinking beer in her mother's backyard.

DYLAN   We can go over to the hospital if you want.

CLAIRE   No, this is where I should be.

DYLAN   But what if your mom's right and your grammy—

CLAIRE   *(interrupts)* No, Mom's just.... Look, Randy's there with her, and her brothers.... And Grammy's, like, sleeping anyway. *(kisses him)* There's no cake.

DYLAN   It's not like it's my *tenth* birthday. *(beat)* How'd that ever start, d'ya think, I mean, sticking burning candles in your food?

CLAIRE   *(shrugs)* Google it. Mom did tell me to say "happy birthday." But then, of course, she *had* to inform me that turning twenty-one was *such* a bigger deal in *her* day.

DYLAN   Oh, they think everything was a bigger deal in *their* day. Frickin' boomers.

CLAIRE   It was weird, 'cause it was the first time ever that Grammy didn't say, "*You* had it easy. I was born in wartime."

DYLAN   Yeah, well, she's going to die in wartime, too.

CLAIRE   Dylan! Come on! That's just so.... Don't be so...

DYLAN   What—matter of fact? So we should *all* be talking in euphemisms? Like Laurel's fucking family?

     An uneasy moment.

     Wartime. Hey, there's a word for you.

CLAIRE   Word? Isn't it a phrase?

DYLAN   *(with an edge of mimicry)* Google it. *(beat)* Sorry.

> *Another uneasy moment.*

> But, the most privileged generation in the history of the world *ever*, and they were going to change *everything*—so why are we in fucking Afghanistan?

CLAIRE   All right!

DYLAN   *(beat)* Where does Google come from? I mean the word?

CLAIRE   *(shrugs)* Doesn't it come from Barney?

DYLAN   *Barney?*

CLAIRE   Barney Google. There was an old song Grammy used to sing. "Barney Google, with the goo-goo-googley eyes..." That's the only other place I ever heard it.

DYLAN   Barney Google?

CLAIRE   Yeah. With the goo-goo-googley eyes.

DYLAN   *(beat)* You should Google that.

CLAIRE   Google *Google?*

DYLAN   Google google. Putsy wootsie mushie wooshie kishsy wishsy— *(kisses her)* I am sorry. I know how much you love your grammy.

> *After a moment, she begins to sing quietly, more to herself than to him.*

CLAIRE   *(sings)* "Barney Google with the goo-goo-googley eyes Barney Google had a wife three times his size..."

DYLAN   Remember when Laurel won that thing in track, that provincial thing? She was so fast, she was so.... Like the newspaper even talked about the Olympics. But now her stupid parents are all like they raised her to be this hero and get killed.

CLAIRE   Dyl—

DYLAN   Like they're being scripted by the PMO or NATO or... *(mimics)* "We just talked to her the other night and she believed in what she was doing, she said she didn't want to be anywhere else on earth." *Right.* Like she wanted to be blown to shit.

CLAIRE   Please, you have to stop, Dyl, you have to— Look, you know that she phoned Peter last week, too, like out of the blue, so he's really fucked up and—

DYLAN   Oh man, it's all so... so.... Like, why did they have to have that stupid fight and break up?

CLAIRE   I know. But they wanted different things. And then the army was her idea, nobody made her do it. They couldn't stay together because *you* wanted them to. Or me. Or even Pete. *(beat, then she sings, changing the subject)* "Goo-goo-googley..." That stupid dinosaur has forever ruined that name now *forever.*

DYLAN   What name?

CLAIRE   *Barney.*

DYLAN   Oh. I think Barney Rubble ruined it first.

CLAIRE   Oh, right. Oh, and I suppose Barney Google ruined it before that, really.

DYLAN   *(beat)* When was the first time you realized that you were going to die?

CLAIRE   What? Oh, aren't you just a big bundle of birthday joy.

DYLAN   That girl who was in grade eleven the year we started grade ten. Remember her? Betty or Barbie or some B name. That anorexic girl a year ahead of us.

CLAIRE   It was a D name. Denny. B is for Barney.

DYLAN   Right, Denny. Denise. It blew me away that she just like, died. "We're all gonna die," I thought. Like not right away, but... eventually.

CLAIRE   *(beat)* Dyl—

DYLAN   But Jesus! "The Ultimate Sacrifice!" *Jesus!*

CLAIRE   You can't be mad at Laurel's parents.

DYLAN	Why not? I never liked them anyway, but they're so shameful now, they're just so— I mean, taking the press into her bedroom! Parading her baby pictures, her trophies, her— That picture of her father in the paper hugging that stupid stuffed penguin.
CLAIRE	Pete gave her that penguin.
DYLAN	Oh, Jesus.
CLAIRE	And why can't they? After all, she was their daughter and now she's... she's *gone*.
DYLAN	*Gone?* She's "gone"? Jesus Christ, Claire, she was blown up. Fucking blown to.... Her body must look like someone went apeshit in the meat department at Safeway. They probably scraped her off the pavement, if they even *have* pavement over—
CLAIRE	*Stop!* This is exactly why people have euphemisms.
DYLAN	'Cause they won't face the truth!
CLAIRE	No, 'cause they can't *bear* it.
DYLAN	*(beat)* It just drives me crazy the way that they try to justify being there. I mean, a place where people hate your guts because, because, you're you. A place that isn't like anyplace you know or care about or ever wanted to go.
CLAIRE	I always wanted to go there.
DYLAN	Oh please. Afghanistan? Gimme a break.
CLAIRE	I've always had this thing about Asia. The steppes of Russia.
DYLAN	Steppes are just the stupid Prairies with, like, an exotic name.
CLAIRE	*(beat)* I've been going to Google Earth.

> DYLAN *laughs.*

What's funny?

DYLAN	That sounds so strange. "I've been going to Google Earth." Like it's a place. Like a real imaginary place, like *Middle* Earth.
CLAIRE	Okay...
DYLAN	My friend Barney and I have been going to— *(beat)* Sorry. So you've been going to Google Earth?
CLAIRE	Yeah. And after the hospital this afternoon with Mom and Gram, I just kept flying all over the place: here and Kandahar and— You think like Google Earth is this one big picture of the whole world, but really it's all these satellite pieces stuck together. Like, have you ever looked at Edmonton? Closely? It's summer mostly, green trees and— But just south of where my dad and his girlfriend live, down past Mill Woods? There's snow there. As if you could walk across the street and be in another year. *(beat)* So I went and found Laurel's parents' house.
DYLAN	Why?
CLAIRE	I don't know. 'Cause she was killed, I guess. And then I typed in Kandahar. And, like, *bang*, it zooms up into outer space and flies to Afghanistan. And I'm thinking, when were the satellites taking all these pictures? Are we down there on Whyte Ave.? Like, little specks? And Afghanistan—was this when they were being fucked over by the Russians, or when the Taliban was in power? Is Osama bin Laden down there somewhere? A little dot with his gang in a cave, like the forty thieves in *Ali Baba*.
DYLAN	Selfish millionaire prick.
CLAIRE	But I know for sure that I'm looking at Afghanistan before Laurel went there, before she was—
	PETER arrives.
PETER	Hey.
CLAIRE	Hey Pete.

DYLAN	S'up?
PETER	I thought you'd be at the hospital.
CLAIRE	(*shakes her head*) Mom said she'll call if...
PETER	Who's there now?
CLAIRE	Uncle Dave and Uncle Bill, and your dad.
PETER	Okay. I think I'll go over.
CLAIRE	Grammy won't even know if you're there probably, like even if she's awake. Dolly phoned from Toronto, and she didn't know who it was anymore. And they like always talk on the phone every morning, those two. Where've you been?

> PETER *shrugs.*

DYLAN	Have a beer? A birthday beer?
PETER	Your birthday?
DYLAN	Twenty-one.
PETER	Sure. (*He takes a beer, toasts.*) Happy birthday.
CLAIRE	Where'd you go last night?
PETER	(*beat*) I went over to see Laurel's folks.
DYLAN	Yeah?

> CLAIRE *gives* DYLAN *a look.*

I'm so sorry man, I'm so.... It really sucks, she was great. She was... (*shrugs*)

PETER	Yeah.
CLAIRE	How was it?
PETER	Their house feels all different. Like not going to a house but more like, I don't know, church or... it's all formal and quiet. Melissa won't come out of her room, and Billy's all fucked up.
DYLAN	Billy always was fucked up.

PETER	Yeah, but he's worse. And their dad. It's just.... Oh, boy, he just hugged me and hugged me and cried. It's strange to try and comfort a man, like a big, bald, porky man. And we never even liked each other before!
CLAIRE	I'm glad you went there. We haven't had much to do with them for a couple of years, I mean, not since you two broke up, and after something terrible like this, then...
PETER	Yeah. I just kept patting his back. Like he was some kind of big dog or something. *(beat)* Did Claire tell you that she phoned me? That Laurel phoned me?
DYLAN	Yeah man, she did. Wow.
PETER	Yeah.
DYLAN	How long did you talk or...?
PETER	Not long. Like maybe ten minutes? She just phoned she said because she was homesick and thinking of home and...
DYLAN	Did she say what it was like there or...?
PETER	A little. *(beat)* Hey Clairy, there's something...
CLAIRE	What?
PETER	I signed up.
CLAIRE	For what?
PETER	Like I enlisted.
DYLAN	You stupid fuck!
PETER	Hey—
CLAIRE	Shut up, Dyl! You *what*?
PETER	I've been thinking about it. I don't want to go back to university. What do I care about all that shit? And I hate my job, it sucks so much.
CLAIRE	Mom is going to flip out.

PETER   I know. So don't tell her just yet. Not with Grammy and...

CLAIRE   And your dad. Jesus.

PETER   Yeah, right, I know. It's kind of fucked.

DYLAN   You just decided to go and do this? Without talking to anybody?

CLAIRE   Dylan!

PETER   I talked to Laurel's dad.

DYLAN   Oh, Jesus, that's really fucked.

PETER   *Look, shithead–*

DYLAN   But Laurel's dad? Mr. Come Take Pictures of My Dead Daughter's Bedroom? That's the *stupidest fucking thing I–*

PETER   Hey–

CLAIRE   *Shut up, Dyl! Shut up, shut up!*

DYLAN   *No, you shut up, you fucking–*

                  A moment.

              Happy fuckin' birthday!

                  He grabs his beer and storms off.

CLAIRE   Dyl!

                  He's gone. She stands, unsure of what to do.

PETER   Oh Clairy...

                  She looks at her brother.

              Everything used to be so, so... easier.

                  Lights fade and cross to the next scene.

Scene 2: 1970

Edmonton, an early summer afternoon by the river.

JOANNE, DEBBI, and RANDY burst into view, laughing. DEBBI comes on first, a knapsack in her hand. RANDY is moving as fast as he can, but JOANNE is hanging onto him, her arms and legs wrapped around his leg. He drags her along. He also has a guitar slung over his shoulder. His T-shirt is off and hanging from the belt of his jeans.

JOANNE	Giddy-up, giddy-up, giddy—
DEBBI	Hurry up!
RANDY	How? I've got a parasite!
DEBBI	A what?
JOANNE	What'd you call me, pardner?
RANDY	A parasite!
JOANNE	Like the clap!
DEBBI	The clap isn't a parasite!
JOANNE	I meant crabs. Like the crabs!
RANDY	Let go of me, Crab Woman!
JOANNE	No! I'd rather be Clap Woman! Watchit! Here she comes!

JOANNE lets go of RANDY and lies on the ground.

	Like a clap out of the blue! It's Clap Woman!
DEBBI	That's bolt out of the blue, numbnuts.
JOANNE	Here she comes! Faster than a—than a— *(giggles)*
DEBBI	Let's stop here for the night, men.
RANDY	Who wants a toke?
DEBBI	Oh God, no more, Randy, no. And don't give her any more.

> *JOANNE is rolling back and forth on the ground, chanting to Rossini's "William Tell Overture" and clapping in time.*

JOANNE   To the clap, to the clap, to the clap-clap-clap
          To the clap, to the clap, to the clap-clap-clap
          To the clap, to the clap, to the clap-clap-clap
          CLAAAAP TO THE CLAP-CLAP-CLAP!

RANDY   I could use a toke.

JOANNE   Clap Woman! Faster than a speeding bullet!

DEBBI   Oh God—

JOANNE   Clap Woman! Don't even speak her name! Just applaud and she'll know you're calling to her! "Help me! Oh help me!"

> *JOANNE applauds wildly and giggles. RANDY starts to clap as well.*

RANDY   I need assistance!

> *JOANNE jumps to her feet.*

JOANNE   Do not panic, never fear
          The woman with the Clap is here!

RANDY   *(beat)* Seriously, this one's already rolled.

DEBBI   Like we need any more?

JOANNE   I don't know, I feel pretty straight.

DEBBI   Put it away, Randy—more later.

JOANNE   What I could really use are some snacks. I am so hungry all of a sudden!

> *DEBBI pulls a bag of popcorn from her knapsack.*

DEBBI   Start in on this.

JOANNE   Yay!

> *They eat.*

What a good day this is. I am having such a *good* day!

RANDY	Goody.
DEBBI	Me too. It's like.... You know the games that kids teach each other, the ones that your parents have nothing to do with? It's like that.
RANDY	What?
DEBBI	You know, hopscotch and hide-and-seek and—
JOANNE	Skipping rhymes!
RANDY	One potato, two potato, three potato, four—
DEBBI	Like that!
RANDY	Five potato, six potato—
ALL THREE	Seven potato, MORE!
JOANNE	Kids are still doing that, aren't they?
RANDY	Huh?
JOANNE	That world is still there, going on without us. Eight-year-olds passing things on to six-year-olds. No one tells them to, no one makes them. It's just a world that they make for themselves and always have. I want to go back to that.
RANDY	To being six?
JOANNE	No, to not being, not being—oh, to not being *forced* to *conform* to our parents' generation's idea of, of—oh—of the way they want us to conform to all that conformation bullshit!
DEBBI	What's pathetic is that I can understand what Clap Woman is saying.
RANDY	Heavy. *(beat)* What else do you have in that bag?
	DEBBI takes out more food, bottles of things to drink.
JOANNE	Yummy.

They begin to have a picnic. While DEBBI and JOANNE deal with the food, RANDY starts to fool around with his guitar.

My brothers are so respect-tic-a-bull. They went into business because they understand how much everybody suffered during the Great Depression. They are ants! We are grasshoppers! Not aunts like my father's sisters, the Ukrainian aunts. But wouldn't you rather be a grasshopper? My mother was an only child and didn't provide me with any aunts of the maternal order. *(beat)* If we went to Vancouver, we could find more people like us.

RANDY   What do you mean, like us?

DEBBI   Joanne thinks we're hippies.

RANDY   Oh. *(beat)* Aren't we?

JOANNE   Vancouver would be so cool. So... un-prairie like, so un-flat. Failing that, I think we should move into that house in Garneau.

DEBBI   My parents would have a bird.

JOANNE   But you're twenty-one! Almost.

DEBBI   You forget my parents are older than yours.

JOANNE   No they're not. Mine were born in World War I! They are practically the oldest parents in the English-speaking entire world!

           RANDY starts to play a few chords.

           We could call it "The Freak House"!

DEBBI   Joanne, no. My father'd disown me.

JOANNE   Then let's go to Vancouver and sing. Presenting "Ge-tar Man and the Clap Sisters."

DEBBI   Oh, that sounds way hip.

JOANNE	But you've got to stand up and– Oh, Deb, why didn't you come! You should've come, you should've come! Right, Randy? She should've come.

RANDY plays, they listen.

RANDY	Vancouver would be cool, but San Francisco.... *Wow.*
DEBBI	*America?* I don't think so.
RANDY	But it's not like America in San Francisco, it's a whole other, other–
JOANNE	Janis Joplin. In Calgary! I still can't believe you. We're there–right, Randy?–and she's–she's–*every-thing,* and I'm thinking, Deb is missing this because she's *filing?* Because she's back home *filing* for the federal government?
DEBBI	You keep saying this like I didn't *want* to go. Look, Joanne, I'd've lost my job.
JOANNE	So what? In Calgary! Janis. *Joplin!* Jesus.
RANDY	The music from San Francisco will *save* America.
DEBBI	What? Oh, brother. Go tell that to the Vietnamese.
RANDY	But it will, it–
DEBBI	Or those poor slobs at Kent State, shot dead on the way to class. No way I'd ever move to the States these days, no way in hell. They voted for *Nixon!*
RANDY	But it's our, our... *(He can't quite think of the word.)*
DEBBI	Our what?
RANDY	Our... *mission!* Yes. It is our mission to make San Francisco even more... *un-America.* Because ever since Expo we are, we are so, so...
DEBBI	We *who?*
JOANNE	*(starts singing like girl group back-up singer)* We-who we-who/
RANDY	Canadians.

JOANNE	We-ooo we-ooo...
DEBBI	Like *who*, exactly?
RANDY	Like Neil Young, and—
JOANNE	Joni Mitchell. And most of the guys in Joplin's band, in her new band!
RANDY	And most of the Band, I mean the *Band* band, like Rick Danko and Robbie Robertson and—
JOANNE	And that Halifax guy from the Mamas and the Papas—
DEBBI	*(I rest my case.)* And Leonard Cohen.
JOANNE	Oh here we go.
RANDY	What?
DEBBI	It's the *truth.* Leonard Cohen spent the winter *here* and he wrote "Sisters of Mercy" *here* for two girls who used to know my cousin Patty. And it's also an acknowledged *fact* that they introduced the *miniskirt* to *Edmonton.* The girls, I mean, not Leonard Cohen.
JOANNE	She always brings that up like it's a reason to stay here. Is Leonard Cohen still here? No. He's in Greece or...
RANDY	*(He's figured it out.)* Canadians are the catalyst for the music that will save America from itself.
DEBBI	Oh, man. Where'd we find this guy?
RANDY	Look, Neil Young had this band called the Squires, right? And one night in Winnipeg he meets Stephen Stills, who's on tour? And it was, you know, *Wow, man, we have to play together*, and then they go their separate ways—but then a year later they had this *incredible* second meeting in *California* on a *freeway* with opposite directions and tires screeching and U-turns 'cause Stills recognizes his hearse, right? 'Cause Neil Young drives this hearse. And so they get together and they start Buffalo Springfield.

Meanwhile, in San Francisco, Roger McGuinn and David Crosby were with the Byrds, right? And while all that's happening—this is *so* cool—in England, Graham Nash is with the Hollies? But then, this alignment thing begins: Crosby leaves the Byrds, Nash leaves the Hollies and they get together with Stills and they start Crosby, Stills, and Nash—

JOANNE   It's like the Bible.

DEBBI   What?

JOANNE   Like in the Bible—they *begat*. They get together and begat Crosby, Stills, and Nash!

RANDY   Heavy. But then, catalyst time, the Canadian—

JOANNE   They begat Crosby, Stills, Nash, and *Young*!

RANDY   Right! And then *they* begat *Déjà Vu*, that fine, fine album—

JOANNE   Wow.

> RANDY *is playing Crosby, Stills, Nash, and Young's* "Our House."

DEBBI   *(giggles)* You two are so fulla shit.

> RANDY *sings the chorus of* "Our House."

JOANNE   *(over)* I think the three of us should move into that house. *(beat)* Wait, wait, *wait!*

> RANDY *stops.*

DEBBI   What?

JOANNE   Wow. I just. I just had this— Together, the three of us, we make up this complete thing.

RANDY   Huh?

JOANNE   Body, Heart, and Mind.

DEBBI   What?

JOANNE   *(to DEBBI)* You are the Mind. *(to RANDY)* And Randy, you are the Body.

JOANNE suddenly kisses him.

You are such a good kisser!

RANDY   I've been practising.

> *They kiss again. DEBBI shifts her body a little apart from them.*

JOANNE   Deb, come see what a good kisser he is!

DEBBI   What?

JOANNE   C'mere.

> *RANDY kisses DEBBI.*

RANDY   Wow.

DEBBI   This is a little freaky.

JOANNE   Not nearly as freaky as our parents in their comfortable, comfortable, never-questioning authority—we can be honest. We can be—

DEBBI   Careful now—

JOANNE   I don't want to get married and live in Bonnie Doon. I don't want a Mixmaster. My brothers with their wives and their jobs like ants— Why can't we be freaks and go on like this forever? When we get to be old, we'll live together in Haight-Ashbury in a big house for old grasshoppers.

> *JOANNE kisses RANDY. When she pulls back, she watches him kiss DEBBI.*

You are the best people. I love you both so much!

> *RANDY reaches out for her.*

I am so happy!

Scene 3: 1939

Toronto. A small stage in a hotel. A Saturday night in summer.

A small band plays and HELEN sings "Let's Fall in Love" by Harold Arlen and Ted Koehler. She's standing in a spotlight and wearing a spangly dress; her friend DOLLY stands nearby.

HELEN sings the chorus first, and then, when she begins the introduction, she is joined by DOLLY, singing a lovely harmony. There's a connection between the two: it's clear that they love singing together.

While they sing the final verse, snow slowly begins to fall like confetti.

Scene 4: 1917

January, Flanders, late afternoon. JAMIE, PAUL, and MAC are in a trench. Snow is falling.

PAUL	Oh, I love kissing, and she loves being kissed. *(beat)* But she was shy, at first, you know, she was... *(winks, whispers)* She was shy of my tongue.
MAC	Why, is it forked?
PAUL	*(laughs)* Idiot. No, she's a nice girl, Bernadette. I had to proceed slowly, and with determination—but gentle. It was patient, patient work. Because, well, at first she thought such a thing was common, was— She's a good girl, never misses a Mass and studies piano with the nuns.
MAC	Oh, we know all about those loose Catholic girls, eh Jamie? Priests get 'em all warmed up for—
PAUL	*(quickly, violently)* Fuck off!
MAC	What—

PAUL	I don't have to take that crap from you!
MAC	Paul, I didn't mean—
PAUL	I have to take it from these goddamn superior—they think they...
MAC	Just being silly, I'm...
PAUL	(beat) Sorry, Mac, sorry.
MAC	I didn't mean...
PAUL	I know. (beat) It's a fine way to welcome a friend from home. I'm sorry.
MAC	That's all right. I didn't— I'm sorry.
	An awkward moment.
JAMIE	(beat) It's pretty. The snow.
PAUL	It'll hide the misery for a few minutes.
JAMIE	Snow like this always makes everything so quiet.
PAUL	But it's not cold enough to freeze. So more mud.
JAMIE	Is it snowing back home, I wonder? Sarah and the baby are probably still with her folks.
PAUL	Mac, you must have some news. Tell me something about somebody back there.
MAC	Like who?
PAUL	Anybody. The letters I get aren't very newsy, Bernadette mostly writes about us, and all my mother ever says is, "Don't worry about me," and "Nothing ever happens here."
MAC	Well, nothing much does—it's Moncton.
JAMIE	(beat) I still can't get over—that is, they're right there.
MAC	Where'd you think they'd be?
JAMIE	Not this close! (beat) I can't get over it!

PAUL	You'll get over it soon enough. *(beat)* At night sometimes you can hear them snore. One of them that was there for a while—so loud! Like being downstairs and hearing my old man up in the bedroom. *(beat)* No, we pretty much live with Fritz.
JAMIE	They can hear us talking?
PAUL	Depends on the wind. Don't think they don't always know where you are though. There's a sniper there just ready for you.
MAC	*(beat)* Back home—remember when we were out at the back of your yard and we could hear old Mrs. Ross through her window?
PAUL	Oh, that's right, that time! *(laughs)*
MAC	Jamie, you wouldn't know who we're talking about. She was an old widow and tiny, a scrawny wee thing, sweet as pie, wouldn't say boo, and this morning we're out playing in Paul's yard and we heard this noise, like somebody moaning in pain—

> *PAUL moans in mock pain.*

"Listen," I says, someone's hurt somewhere.

> *PAUL moans.*

So we go back to the fence—this big old board fence—we know it's coming from the other side. And this one says, "It's a girl!"

> *PAUL makes a falsetto moan.*

Then she goes—

PAUL	"Oh, oh, oh!"
MAC	And we're twelve or ten or something and dirty-minded so we think we're hearing some girl, you know, having... relations.
PAUL	"Oh! Oh!"

MAC	But there's this noise, like a shot from a gun, I swear!
PAUL	*BAM!* A blast! Like a bomb!
MAC	And we realize it's her, old lady Ross and her bathroom window is open—
PAUL	She's having a big, noisy poop!
JAMIE	No!
PAUL	That turd must have been as big as she was!
MAC	We couldn't look at her without laughing after that. And it was worse for me—I had to see her every week at church. She taught me Sunday school.
PAUL	We were so bad.
MAC	BAM!
PAUL	*(beat)* What part of town are you from?
JAMIE	We have a little place there on Mountain Road. Sarah and I moved up from Nova Scotia after we got married. You lived near Mac?
PAUL	On the other side of North Street.
MAC	Fellows, I'm going to try and have a little snooze.
	He moves aside, keeping his head down.
PAUL	Mac? Sorry to jump down your throat before.
MAC	Don't think about it.
PAUL	It's good to see a familiar face.
	The snow has stopped.
JAMIE	*(beat)* I'm too keyed up to sleep.
PAUL	Bet you wished now you'd never signed up.
JAMIE	If I'd known at the time we were going to have a baby... *(shrugs)*
PAUL	How old?

JAMIE	She's born in November.
PAUL	So you've never seen her?
JAMIE	No. *(beat)* You two were good chums back home.
PAUL	We were, yes. Your cousin was my best friend until we were in high school or so. We had a lot of fun. *(beat)* A lot of fun.
JAMIE	And you've been over here more than a year?
PAUL	That's right.
JAMIE	*(beat)* You hear things, you know, about what it's like. But then to see it. To see...
PAUL	You'll get used to it.
JAMIE	I don't know how. *(beat)* Last week, the first day we were here, I was with this fellow from Shubenacadie– Bert Mackenzie, Albert, nice fellow, we got to know each other on the way over. All excited about it, great adventure, and just nineteen, had his birthday in London. "Happiest day of my life," he says. We went to see that *Chu Chin Chow* show at the theatre.
PAUL	That's somethin, eh? That market in Baghdad? Ali Baba and those slave girls?
JAMIE	Yeah. *(beat)* But the first day we get near the front, he's walking up ahead of me and the next thing, there's a sound coming at us–whizbang–and he blows apart. Just... gone.
PAUL	Didn't even know what hit him probably.
JAMIE	And there's... well, bits of him on me. Bits of... oh Jesus.
PAUL	Puts a stop to that old adventure horseshit don't it?
JAMIE	To see someone go like that, someone you know, and so close by me. I don't see how I could ever get used to that.

PAUL	The worst of it is you will. Have to or you can't function. This fuckin' thing has to end at some point— but right now that seems damn impossible. After a while, it's hard to believe there ever was anything else.
JAMIE	But he didn't even get to fight!
PAUL	Jamie, the terrible thing is, it's nothing special over here. If it happened back home, everything'd stop. If someone got killed like that in Moncton, people wouldn't be able to stop talking about it. But here, after a while, it's nothing special. Happens everywhere, all over the place, sometimes umpteen hundreds of us in a single day.
JAMIE	But I can't let him just— I just—
PAUL	Maybe you should write a letter to his folks, tell them what a fine lad he was and a good pal to you.
JAMIE	But I don't want them to know how terrible... how...
PAUL	I used to wonder if the stupid idiots in charge of this thing have any sense of it. Sitting and looking at maps in the war office, if they really knew, would they send us here? And I've come to a sad conclusion.
JAMIE	Yes?
PAUL	They know, that's the worst of it. But they also know that they're better than we are. I jumped down poor Mac's throat there 'cause here, this morning, just before you fellows arrived, I had to listen to some high and mighty Anglican snot officer talk about "the superiority of the Protestant soldier." And I think, we risk our stupid necks, the very least we can expect is to be treated decent-like by our own side. When I go back to London on leave, snotty fart bastards there look at me like I'm nothing, like, "Who do you think you are?"

JAMIE	*(beat)* But London. I never thought I'd ever see such a place. To see those things from school days—the Tower and London Bridge.
PAUL	And the slave girls in that show.
JAMIE	For a while there I was thinking that I'm the luckiest fellow alive to be able to see such sights! "I hope the war doesn't end before I've seen it all!" I thought.
PAUL	It's like there's a big party goin' on there all the time. And at first that's a great thing, you think, normal life, and maybe a girl to take your mind off things. Even if you have to pay her for it. But then that comes to seem more unreal than this does. I'm walking in Piccadilly and I just want to knock someone's head off. And that's not what I— Back home, never was in a fight, never. *(beat)* I realize that I'm relieved when it's time to get back here, back with the boys who understand what this is. But how stupid can you get? *(beat)* Like I said, you get used to it. Everything else becomes more or less unbearable.
JAMIE	*(beat)* What'll we be like when we get back home do you think?
PAUL	Well, aren't you the little optimist! That poor bastard from Shubenacadie is one of the lucky ones maybe. His problems are over.
JAMIE	Bert told me he signed up because of his brother, because his brother wanted to sign up so bad and they wouldn't take him on account of his bad feet.
PAUL	They'll be signin' up the lame by this time next year. They'll be signin' up the sick and the blind. There'll be conscription any day I wager.
JAMIE	Think so?
PAUL	Can't kill us fast enough. Have to replace us somehow. Sometimes I even think those fellows in Quebec are the smart ones—the ones against conscription.

JAMIE	Who's side are you on?
PAUL	Ours—yours and mine and Mac's.
JAMIE	And the Empire?
PAUL	Pah. I'm here for the lads who are in this with me, like your poor friend. *(beat)* When we go back home, how can we even talk about this? Will it mean anything to anyone who isn't us?
JAMIE	What about your girl?
PAUL	I think so much about Bernadette. She writes me, and says she'll wait for me. But what good would I be to her?
JAMIE	You could kiss her.
PAUL	*(laughs)* Yes. I'm in a pissy black mood today, ain't I? *(beat)* Yes, I could kiss her. She was so shy at first. Oh, I love kissing her!
JAMIE	Sarah doesn't like that either. The tongues, I mean. She won't do that.
PAUL	You can persuade her.
JAMIE	Not so far. Not in two years.
PAUL	Look. You go at it like this. First you kiss her all around her mouth, her cheeks and chin. Little gentle baby kisses. *(kiss-kiss-kiss sounds)* Tickle the end of her nose with your tongue, just once, to make her giggle. Then whisper something silly like "bow wow" in her ear and say you're her little puppy.
JAMIE	Oh, now—
PAUL	Her little kissing puppy. No, listen, you make it a game. You have fun with her. And oh, then, gently, gently, you lick her lips—so soft!—lick them, and tickle them with your tongue, and then they'll open, like a little door to heaven, such a tender door, and when your tongue slips inside, then she'll—

JAMIE	Oh stop, Paul, it's...
PAUL	What?
JAMIE	It's too, too...
PAUL	Mac, your cousin's damn shy there, for a married man.

> MAC *doesn't move.*

	Must be asleep. *(beat)* I feel bad about barking at him there. He was just being silly.
JAMIE	He's a fine fellow, cousin Mac.
PAUL	Yes.
JAMIE	*(beat)* At the train station, last time I saw Sarah, he stood in front of us, his back to us. My folks were there, too, but this was later 'cause my father had to take my mother away. Crying so bad, and there was always something with her and Sarah, she...
PAUL	"No girl will ever be good enough for *my* boy."
JAMIE	Yes, something like that I suppose. My father took her home. Then it was Mac there with the two of us, so he said, "Make pretend I'm not here," and turned around. We were against the station wall and he stood there in front of us, to give us some privacy. I kissed her. I go back over it time and again. How long were we there? Maybe a minute or two? But I can stretch it out forever. I can go over it, each second, over and over. *(beat)* The baby there between us, not yet a baby, not born, but there, with us. Mac's back was so close, just— *(With his fingers he indicates a couple of inches.)* and the stone wall, we were in a space between them. She was so close to me. Closer than we had ever been together out in public like that. You know, the way your mother or father is close and big when you're small and they lift you up? And we were kissing and whispering at the same time. When I reached inside her coat, and she took

my hand, and guided it. She had told me that she was so warm with the baby that her clothes made her irritable sometimes—I realized that beneath her coat—

PAUL   *(whispers)* She was bare naked!

JAMIE   No. *(laughs)* But there was nothing beneath her blouse. I felt her, felt her skin, so tight where she had been so soft before, like a drum, you know, and there, beneath her skin, inside of her, the baby moving— I can't begin to tell you what it was like. The station and Mac all disappear and it's almost like we were in the bedroom on Mountain Road and—I'd been in Valcartier at camp, I hadn't seen her so big and—I wanted to be alone someplace with her, to press myself close. Put my ear against her and listen. Mac's shielding us so that we could kiss I imagine he thought, but we were all caught up in what was happening inside her. It was so, so— I don't know how to talk about it, Paul. I don't know what to say or— For there's something unnatural about it. I know that sounds foolish but there it is. About having another thing grow inside of her. Unnatural is wrong, I mean, not real, somehow. Like a magic story. And I thought, "I'm not a kid anymore," and I thought about how hard it would be for her with me away from her for a few months. If only that moment could be stretched and stretched, long enough for the baby to be born and be held and...

PAUL   And?

JAMIE   And she is now. Helen. If it was a girl we decided to call her Helen.

> MAC *begins to snore, beginning with a loud snort. His head is back, his mouth wide open. They watch him and laugh. Then* JAMIE *tosses a bit of food towards his mouth. He does this two or three times, laughing. Then* MAC *starts, sits up.*

MAC   What? What?

> *They laugh. MAC is still dozy. He starts to stand.*

PAUL   Get down, Mac!

> *There is an intense flash of light. MAC's face is suddenly drenched in blood. Gunfire.*

JAMIE   Mac!

> *Blackout.*

Scene 5: 2006

> *Edmonton, late at night, darkness. DYLAN is sitting on the floor. He lights a candle.*
>
> *He opens a newspaper, takes out a page, and starts folding along the edges of a picture and an article, slowly and deliberately. He then starts to tear carefully along the folds. He mistakenly rips a corner of the picture.*

DYLAN   (*whispers*) Shit.

> *He finishes and looks at the ragged-looking clipping.*

Fucking penguin. (*beat*) Fucking stupid Barney Google penguin!

> *He suddenly crumples the clipping, then holds it to the candle flame and begins to quietly sing a wordless "Happy Birthday."*

Bada dada da da
Bada dada da da
Bada daada da dada—

> *Lights are fading as the paper catches fire and burns. He drops it just as it begins to burn his fingers.*

Ow. Shit.

> *He blows out the candle.*

Scene 6: 1894

Northeastern Nova Scotia, a farm. Early in the morning, before sunrise, July.

The figure of a young woman is very gradually revealed, DORA. She is quite pregnant. She has a broom, and is sweeping the snow. Birdsong is heard. She turns in the direction of the sound and listens. Suddenly her hand goes to her belly.

DORA   Oh!

Go ahead. It doesn't hurt.

Kick and kick and kick—

Toss your wee fists against me, yes.

It's when you stop, I get frightened.

Birdsong.

Listen! It's Mr. Robin. Wouldn't you like to wake up in the world every morning and hear that?

The baby kicks. She laughs.

What if we was like that and laid our babies inside eggs? What a great large egg you'd have to be! And what a silly thing I'd look like sitting on that.

And what a silly thing I am to think such a thing. It's no wonder they all lose patience with me. "Go down and sleep in the kitchen," your father says to me, "I'm black and blue from you thrashing around all night!" All I remember when I woke up is that I was running away from something wild from out in the woods.

But you feel so hearty. Much heartier than the *first* one, the girl— "Ruth" I called her, because I love that story. My mother told it to me, time and again. The part when Ruth says to Naomi, "For whither thou goest, I will go; and where thou lodgest, I will lodge: thy people shall be my people, and thy God my

God." And I'll tell you that story, too, I promise. Just be a good baby and live.

But you feel like you've got the fists of a boy—no name like Ruth for you, ruffian. I'll call you James, yes, because he counselled patience. And because that is your uncle's name, too, your father's brother, and we should curry his favour.

But maybe you've got the fists of a girl like my great-grandmother. She was a tough one, they say. And my father was the apple of her eye. He named me for her, his grandmother, Dora Ann. Your great-great-grandmother. Father says that she kept the family going when this was still a wild place before civilization come, when there was nothing but savages and wild animals. "Here we will build us a house and make the best." That's what she said.

If you are hearty like she was, well, just imagine your life for she lived way up in her eighties. She lived in two centuries, Old Dora.

And so will we, God willing. And if you live as long as her, you'd live till... nineteen hundred and eighty... something. Imagine. And your children might live in a century that starts with a two, not a one. The twenty-first, it'll be. And she was born in the eighteenth century. And I'm in the middle, looking forwards and back.

"Here we will build us a house."

And I'm like a house myself, aren't I, with you living inside of me, a house of flesh and blood—

You must not die! Don't follow your poor sister. Ruth was born before sunrise, and gone before midday. She was too tiny, like a bird.

And already you've outlived the other one, who must have loved heaven so much that this earth had no appeal at all.

"Don't look, now," my mother says to me.

"Why not—what's it look like?"

"It looks like nothing," she says, "It wasn't all that far along." And she wrapped it up in a cloth and took it away in a basin.

But you'll be born fat and happy and fully formed. You won't be like wee Ruth and die in my arms. You'll live and be a strapping young fellow or a beautiful girl. Yes! And then your father will not be making me sleep in the kitchen after something chased me in my sleep.

I don't mean to say that your father is unkind or—

But they do lose patience with me.

The very first morning he showed up in church—wasn't he the most handsome thing I'd ever laid eyes upon!

He still is. So you'll be good-looking! That's a good reason to live!

And when I turned and saw him look at me from across the aisle as if I were the single most important being on the entire earth. No one had ever looked at me that way. It was hard to pay attention to my father's sermon for all I could think was, that must be Big Gordon's son Ross home from Halifax and isn't he handsome!

And your father looked at me right there in the church, so bold, and as if we shared a secret. And then the hymn is "Go labour on, spend and be spent"—the one my mother wishes that father would never pick because there's that line at the end that makes the boys snicker—and I only understood why they do because Robbie explained it to me, my sister Roberta who everyone thinks is all innocent and sweet, but she is *not*.

So we're singing and all I can hear is your father's sweet voice. And I can't help but turn, for there he is just across the aisle as close as *(She opens her arms.)* this. And when he reaches the end of the verse, and sings those words that makes the boys snicker, "Soon shalt thou hear the Bridegroom's voice, the midnight peal, 'Behold, I come,'" well, then he winks right at me, right at that moment, and grins at me bold as brass and in such a charming way. It was wicked, I know, but it was so, so—well, are there even words to describe what I felt? Then he spoke to me afterwards out front after church, and no one had ever spoken like that, like—well, like flirting, I suppose you would call it, like somehow he and I were different from all the rest, not so stiff as older folks. New, somehow, modern. He took my breath away.

Oh, I knew it was a sin, but your father said that he loved me so much. Afterwards, that first time—we were in a little dale in the woods—I was frightened and started to cry so he was very tender and silly. He kissed my ear and whispered that he had something important to tell me. "What?" I asked, and he said, "Behold, I come."

And my mother told me that I was a foolish girl and that all that was saving me from disgrace was the position of Ross's father in the church and in the town. That if I had sinned with near anyone else, that father could have disowned me. That if Big Gordon hadn't been such a powerful Orangeman that my life could have been over. So Ross's father and my father took charge and here we are.

But if you live, *all* can be right again. My father would have another grandchild and you would be the apple of his eye maybe, just like he was with his grandmother. And I would love you, and make you so welcome in my life in a way that he could not welcome me in his.

I woke up in the night because something wild was after me—something in the woods, all snarly with teeth—and Ross shaking me, "Wake up, Dora!" he says, "and stop your kicking." And I wish he'd comfort me, maybe, because I was still frightened from the dreaming, but instead he tells me to go sleep in the kitchen. And he says I'm a useless thing and that I tricked him into marriage with poor wee Ruth and I'm good for nothing now. And I know it's because he's working so hard and is so tired and he doesn't want to be working for his father because his older brother's the one who'll inherit it all in the end and here I am waking him up because something's after me in my sleep. I'm just a silly girl, but—

But if you keep kicking, just kick and kick and come kicking right out of me—

Then your father will look at me in that sweet way again, and my own father will truly forgive me for being a wicked girl, for bringing shame upon him and his ministry, and everything, everything, everything, everything will be as happy as—as—

> *The robins' singing is all around her. The pink light of sunrise. She hugs her belly.*

Oh, please!

> *Lights cross to next scene.*

Scene 7: 1870/2006

> *Winter 1870. A house in Pictou County, Nova Scotia. Early afternoon. Also in the scene, another space for 2006.*

> *CLARENCE enters with a Bible; he's reading aloud, but to himself and with an air of uncertainty, as if not quite believing or understanding the words.*

CLARENCE "In sorrow thou shalt bring forth children and thy desire shall be thy husband: and he shall rule over thee."

> *He turns back a page.*

"And the serpent said unto the woman, Ye shall not surely die: For God doth know that in the day ye eat thereof, then your eyes shall be opened and ye shall be as *gods*."

> *A cellphone begins to ring loudly; one of those annoying, cute musical rings, like "La Cucaracha" or "Ode to Joy." CLARENCE is oblivious in his time and space; the sound continues just long enough to make the audience uneasy. He flips forward to a bookmarked text.*

"God of Gods."

> *Then we see CLAIRE, in a light summer nightdress, answering her cellphone.*

CLAIRE Hlo...? What...?

Oh, *Randy*. Hi. No, I thought maybe you'd be Dylan.

How's Grammy?

> *MAUDE enters into the scene with CLARENCE, moving close by CLAIRE as she does.*

MAUDE Why won't that miserable old woman just let go and die!

> *No response from CLARENCE.*

CLAIRE Morphine?

MAUDE She doesn't know who we are or where she is any longer.

CLAIRE So this is *really* it then?

MAUDE And look! Just look!

> *MAUDE shows CLARENCE her forearm; he barely glances at it.*

Our Gram bit me, she did!

CLAIRE   Yeah, okay.

MAUDE   She just *looks* toothless.

CLAIRE   I will. I'll get dressed and come right—

> *She realizes that something major is happening at the other end of the line.*

What? What was that? Was that Mom?

Randy? What happened? Is it Gram, is it—?

Okay, okay. I'll be right—

> *The line goes dead.*

Randy? Ran—

MAUDE   Where's Father?

CLARENCE   Gone for a walk.

MAUDE   He knows better, in this damp.

> *CLAIRE closes her phone; lights begin to fade on her. She's trying not to cry.*

CLAIRE   Fuckit. Damn.

MAUDE   Well, I suppose it means I won't have *him* barking at me for a little bit, and that's some sort of blessing.

> *CLAIRE is no longer seen.*

Our cousins are over there now.

CLARENCE   Clara's arrived?

MAUDE   Yes, just a few moments ago.

> *She examines her arm.*

Gran will never get out of that bed again, but it's as if she's determined to continue making our lives as miserable as her own until the very end. She's back in the Highlands now, with her mother. I don't think there's a word of English left in her. When she's not trying to bite us all, she's screaming out for Flora.

CLARENCE Flora?

MAUDE Her sister, the baby sister who died. Drowned or... something. *That* old story. Seventy or more years ago, that must have been. Biting the living while she's screeching at the dead.

>   CLARENCE *sighs.*

Oh, I should be more charitable, I know. They'll be together soon enough, they will. But she never liked me.

>   CLARENCE *has taken out his pocket watch.*

(teasing) That's some handsome watch, where'd you get that now?

CLARENCE Oh, stop! Maude, just stop!

MAUDE *(beat)* What's— Something's the matter. I know you— something's troubling you. *(beat)* What is it?

CLARENCE *(beat)* Is it possible that God has not revealed things to us, but that we have invented these things?

MAUDE What?

CLARENCE Well, the books of Moses.

MAUDE The books of—*what?*

CLARENCE Genesis, Exodus, Leviticus, Numbers—

MAUDE Deuteronomy, yes I know. Clarence, what are you on about?

CLARENCE "Thou shalt have no other gods before thee," he says. But those others, the ones that God is jealous of! They're written in the Bible as if they were real.

MAUDE You mean Dagon and so forth? The gods of the Philistines and such? What of it? They were uncivilized fools—that's why they're called Philistines!

CLARENCE   No, I mean before that. I mean other gods of the Israelites *themselves.*

MAUDE   Well, they were false gods, silly. And the one true God was revealed over time and history. What are they teaching you in divinity school?

CLARENCE   But if God told Moses that he is the God of *gods,* doesn't that mean there *were* other ones?

MAUDE   I don't—

CLARENCE   *Look,* right here. Deuteronomy 10:17, he says, "For the Lord your God *is* God *of* gods, and Lord *of* lords, *a* great God"—not *the* great God, *a* great God—"*a* great God, *a* mighty, and *a* terrible—" See? *The God of gods.* So he's saying there's more than one.

MAUDE   What's the context for this, silly billy, read me the whole—

CLARENCE   "For the Lord your God *is* God of gods, and Lord of lords, a great God, a mighty, and a terrible which regardeth not persons, nor taketh—"

MAUDE   No, stop, go back, go back and put this in some kind of *context,* please. What comes just before this? Before "For the Lord your God is" and so on? The verse before that?

CLARENCE   Deuteronomy 10:15: "Circumcise therefore the foreskin of your heart, and be no more stiff-necked. For the Lord your God is God of—"

MAUDE   *(interrupting)* Stiff-necked?

CLARENCE   "Be no more stiff-necked." Obstinate, you know.

MAUDE   *(beat) Circumcise* the *foreskin* of your heart?

CLARENCE   Yes.

MAUDE   Don't you think it's possible that this passage could be *slightly* metaphoric?

CLARENCE   Don't make fun of me!

MAUDE   But Clarence—

CLARENCE *(passionately)* I lie awake in the middle of the night and all around there's nothing but dark and.... *Nothing but dark!* We are so alone! I'm so confused and... and.... Are we all alone in a world with no God?

MAUDE   What? Wait. A moment ago there were too many of them and now there's none?

CLARENCE Go ahead, make fun!

MAUDE   I'm not making fun, I—

CLARENCE You never listen, you never, ever listen to me!

MAUDE   I do so! Don't be silly.

CLARENCE *(waves her away)* Forget it. Forget I ever said a thing!

MAUDE   Don't sulk.

CLARENCE It's so *complicated* it's so— It's so *contradictory!* There's two creation stories in Genesis and they contradict each other, there's all these *contradictions!* And it's worse in the Hebrew, you have no idea! I mean even more confusing.

MAUDE   Isn't that why King James translated it to English, so it would make some sense?

CLARENCE Don't be foolish, don't be— Why am I all alone in a dark world where God is hidden from me?

MAUDE   Oh, little brother—

CLARENCE Don't patronize me!

MAUDE   *(beat)* Maybe Father is right after all.

CLARENCE What do you mean?

MAUDE   Perhaps the ministry *isn't* really for you.

CLARENCE *No!*

MAUDE   But maybe you're too... too... sensitive.

CLARENCE	(*barks*) I'm not sensitive!
MAUDE	(*beat*) Have you talked to your teachers of this? Your professors?
CLARENCE	Of course not! And you must say *nothing* to anyone. Most certainly not to Clara, I don't want her to worry with the wedding so close. And Father would only say that he was right all along, that I should stay here and *farm*.
MAUDE	(*beat*) I will.
CLARENCE	Promise!
MAUDE	I promise.
CLARENCE	(*beat*) How's Gran?
MAUDE	How's *Gran*!? She's screaming at the dead and tearing great chunks out of my arm with her tooth!
CLARENCE	You never liked her.
MAUDE	I never liked *her*?
CLARENCE	She used to sing to me.
MAUDE	Oh yes, she doted on you, the youngest. And *male*. On you and our brothers. It was my great misfortune to be the only female born into this family.
CLARENCE	Gran doesn't dislike females.
MAUDE	I'm just that much older than you that I can remember our mother and remember the way that Gran treated her. She's never had any use for anyone of the *female* persuasion.
CLARENCE	She likes Clara.
MAUDE	Everyone likes *Clara*.
CLARENCE	What's that supposed to mean?
MAUDE	Nothing, but that everyone likes her. She's good, she's kind, she's patient, she's generous to a fault, so everyone likes her, even our Gran who has spent her

whole life being mean and ornery to every other female in Creation. You'll be marrying a saint.

CLARENCE   Didn't you get up on the wrong side of bed this morning!

MAUDE   I didn't get up on any side of anything this morning because I've been up all night with a mean old woman who refuses to die!

> *A long moment.*

CLARENCE   She used to hold me in her arms and sing "Ba Ba Mo Leanabh."

MAUDE   She had a lovely singing voice, I'll grant you that. And I believe Father when he says she was a great beauty in her day. *(beat)* It must've been awful leaving everything behind and coming across the ocean. Maybe she's been so hard on me because I've been able to make up my own mind on things, go to normal school and so on. Have a kind of independence that her generation never dreamed possible.

CLARENCE   *(sings quietly)* O ba ba mo leanabh
Ba mo leanabh, ba
O ba ba mo leanabh
Ni mo leanabhs' an Ba Ba.

MAUDE   Clarence, I need you to help me with something, that is...

CLARENCE   What?

MAUDE   Promise me you'll keep this to yourself for the time being?

CLARENCE   Keep what?

MAUDE   I'll not speak of this dark patch you're in with your faith...

CLARENCE   What is it?

MAUDE   *(beat)* We've always been the two closest to each other in the family—close since we lost our mother—

and I would like to... *(beat)* There's a man in Stellarton who I've come to— I've grown very fond of him.

CLARENCE   A man!

MAUDE   Yes, a man. I'm a grown woman even if I am your sister. He works for the mines, above ground, in the office there. I would be well provided for.

CLARENCE   So big sister married.

MAUDE   And with a family.

CLARENCE   A family?

MAUDE   He's a widower, so there's a family already. Two girls and a boy, in fact; five, seven, and eight. Their mother died bringing the youngest.

CLARENCE   Oh. And you like these children?

MAUDE   Very much. They are the reason for it all. We met through them.

CLARENCE   They are your students?

MAUDE   No. The house where I board is next to the street where they live. One of them fell from a tree—nothing serious, but a bloody forehead. As I was walking by. Now, we have discussed this at length and have agreed to do nothing until the school year is over. We both have grave concerns. And I'd have to stop teaching, of course. Forever. Because the law is so idiotic.

CLARENCE   He's a good man?

MAUDE   Yes, good and kind. And very devout. *(beat)* And here's where I would like you to try and understand and to keep your counsel for the time being, and support me. Will you do that?

CLARENCE   What is it?

MAUDE   (*beat*) He would like us to be married in the same
              church where he married his first wife.

CLARENCE   Not married here then.

MAUDE   No, in Antigonish. (*beat*) At St. Ninian's.

CLARENCE   St. Ninian's?

MAUDE   Yes.

CLARENCE   But Maude, that's a Roman church.

MAUDE   Yes, it is.

CLARENCE   Married in a Roman church?

MAUDE   Yes.

CLARENCE   His wife was a Catholic, then?

MAUDE   Yes.

CLARENCE   But—he isn't a *Catholic*? (*beat*) Maude?

MAUDE   Yes.

CLARENCE   How could you even think of such a thing!

MAUDE   I love the man, I love the children. They need
              a mother—

CLARENCE   From their own faith surely!

MAUDE   And I will be that.

CLARENCE   How? (*beat*) No. You'd give up your faith? Become
              a Roman?

MAUDE   Exchanging one way that I worship God for another—
              God is God.

CLARENCE   But the *Pope*! They worship the *Pope*!

MAUDE   They don't worship the Pope! The Pope is God's
              representative on earth.

CLARENCE   It's idolatry and graven images.

MAUDE   The Pope is not a graven image.

CLARENCE   I can't believe it. My own sister, a Roman?

MAUDE   Will you support me when I talk to father? *(beat)*
            Will you help me?

CLARENCE   Don't you dare do anything so disgraceful!

MAUDE   *(beat)* But I have, you see. Already.

CLARENCE   You have? *Married?*

MAUDE   No. Turned. In my heart, I have turned.

CLARENCE   You, here, now, in our father's house, a *Roman
            Catholic?*

            CLARA arrives.

CLARA   *(beat)* It's Gran. She's gone.

CLARENCE   Oh, Clara.

            *CLARA goes to CLARENCE. A rather formal
            embrace.*

CLARA   She was peaceful at the end. I knelt beside the bed
            and asked her how she was. "Happy to be home,"
            she said. "Flora, there you are," she said. "I found
            you, you naughty girl." Her voice was so weak, no
            one could hear her but me. And she was singing,
            when she died, I'm sure of it.

            *While CLARA speaks OLD DORA appears in the
            distance, as a young woman, her hair wild and free.
            She's wearing an old, dirty nightdress.*

OLD DORA   *(whispers)* Flora! Flora!

            *OLD DORA comes to an open coffin sitting on the
            ground. She kneels beside it and looks into it as ten-
            derly as if it were a cradle. She begins to sing as
            CLARA speaks.*

            Flora.

            (sings) O ba ba mo leanabh
            Ba mo leanabh, ba

O ba ba mo leanabh
Nì mo leanabhs' an Ba Ba.

CLARA All the pain and stress seemed to vanish from her face. Mother said, "Look, it's as if she were a girl again." And it was. She looked lovely. (*beat*) And then she gave up the ghost.

> OLD DORA, *still singing, slowly climbs into the coffin and lies down.*

OLD DORA *Eudail mhòir a shluaigh an Dòmhain*
Dhòirt iad d'fhuil an dé;
'S chuir iad do cheann air stob daraich,
Tacan beag bho do chré.

> CLARENCE *is standing between his cousin and his sister.*

MAUDE (*quietly*) Clarence?

> *The singing stops. A moment of silence.*

> CLARENCE *turns to* MAUDE. *He looks as if he is about to burst into tears. Throughout all of this,* MAUDE *is watching her brother.* CLARA *moves towards the coffin. She turns back to* CLARENCE.

CLARA Clarence?

> *Offstage voices can be heard singing.*

> CLARENCE *looks at his sister, then turns away and goes to* CLARA. *The neighbours file on, singing the lament. The men lift the coffin and slowly carry it. The women follow, all singing.*

NEIGHBOURS *O ba ba mo leanabh*
Ba mo leanabh, ba
O ba ba mo leanabh
Nì mo leanabhs' an Ba Ba.

Dhìrich mi Bheinn Mhòr gun anal
Dhìrich agus thearn.

Chuirinn falt mo chinn fo d'chasan
Agus craicionn mo dhà làimh.

> CLARA and CLARENCE are leaving with the
> neighbours. CLARA looks back at MAUDE, unsure
> of what is happening between brother and sister.
> CLARENCE does not look back. As the singing con-
> tinues offstage, MAUDE is left alone.

> While this is happening, as the neighbours leave,
> another figure is revealed standing alone and apart
> from MAUDE. It's CLAIRE, in her nightdress.

O ba ba mo leanabh
Ba mo leanabh, ba
O ba ba mo leanabh
Nì mo leanabhs' an Ba Ba.

CLAIRE   Grammy.

> Suddenly, MAUDE slaps her own face with
> a frightening violence.

MAUDE   You fool. You stupid fool.

CLAIRE   Oh, Grammy, Grammy. I'm so sorry

> Singing continues in the distance.

> Blackout.

> End of Act One.

ACT TWO

Scene 1: 1872

Nova Scotia, a manse in Pictou County.

CLARENCE with a Bible. CLARA arrives behind him as he speaks.

CLARENCE   *(working his way though the text)* "Do not I hate them, O Lord, that hate thee? ... I hate them with perfect hatred: I count them mine enemies." *(beat)* "Search me, O God, and know my heart: try me, and know my thoughts: And see if there be any wicked way in me, and lead me in—"

He sees CLARA.

(startled) You're back.

CLARA   Yes. *(beat)* How was Robbie?

CLARENCE   She's next door, with Mrs. MacPherson.

CLARA   Next door?

CLARENCE   She was crying and I must get this sermon out of the way.

CLARA   So you took her to the neighbours?

CLARENCE   John MacPherson is on the session at the church.

CLARA   So his poor wife is obliged to look after our baby?

CLARENCE   She offered. She doesn't mind, she said. Did my books arrive?

CLARA   They're on the hall table.

CLARENCE   You're a dear, thank you. *(beat)* Sunday's text is Psalm 139.

CLARA   "I will praise thee for I am fearfully and wonderfully made."

CLARENCE   Yes.

CLARA	Isn't that the one with all that "perfect hatred" business?
CLARENCE	Yes, and "Search me oh God and know my heart."
CLARA	*(beat)* Clarence, guess who I saw in town.
CLARENCE	What? Who?
CLARA	Maude, I saw her in town.
CLARENCE	I thought we agreed with Father that we would have nothing whatsoever to do with her.
CLARA	I didn't *speak* with her, dear, I *saw* her. I was coming out from Mrs. Brown's house. She was on the far side of the street and didn't see me. She was with her children—the older one, the boy, was running ahead—doesn't he seem quite the handful! The two girls were with her, and they seem to adore her. And there's a toddler, her own child, I would think. A wee girl.
CLARENCE	No husband in sight?
CLARA	No, but there was a woman with her. I assumed that Maude had come to town to visit his family. Doesn't he have a sister, married to one of the Casey boys?
CLARENCE	Yes, I think so.
CLARA	It was everything I could do not to call out. When we were wee things, how close we were, she and I. And here she was, a few yards away. But she may as well be living in another world.
CLARENCE	She has no one to blame but herself. She knew that Father would disown her.
CLARA	But she hoped that you might help her.
CLARENCE	I don't want to go through this again, Clara. The subject is closed. *(beat)* I have a sermon to finish.
CLARA	Yes. I should go and fetch Roberta.

She moves to leave and then turns back.

	There is something...
CLARENCE	*(impatient)* What *now?*
CLARA	I'm going to have another baby.
CLARENCE	*(not sure how to react)* Oh.
CLARA	Yes. Roberta will have a little brother or sister.
CLARENCE	*(beat)* That's good. *(beat)* That's why you were at Mrs. Brown's, then.
CLARA	Yes.
CLARENCE	Good.
CLARA	*(beat)* And Clarence... I'm going to make up a bed for myself in the back bedroom.
CLARENCE	The back bedroom?
CLARA	Yes.
CLARENCE	I don't understand. Something's amiss? The midwife...?
CLARA	Mrs. Brown says I'm fine—healthy as a horse she says.
CLARENCE	Then...?
CLARA	It's just.... You toss and turn and snore so loudly. I should be sleeping through the nights.
CLARENCE	I see.
CLARA	*(beat)* You've been talking in your sleep.
CLARENCE	So you say.
CLARA	*(beat)* Last night, you were calling for her.
CLARENCE	For who?
CLARA	Maude. In your sleep.
CLARENCE	Oh.
CLARA	Yes. *(beat)* I should relieve poor Mrs. MacPherson. And then there's choir practice to get ready for.

She starts to go.

CLARENCE   Clara?

       She stops and turns to him.

CLARA   Yes?

CLARENCE   *(beat)* I was dreaming. *(beat)* Last night.

CLARA   Yes?

CLARENCE   *(beat)* I was mid-sermon... a Sunday in winter—no heat in the church for some reason and the congregation all wrapped in blankets—and... and they were no longer listening to me—they were watching something else, something *behind* me. And I turn, and... there she is, my sister. In the choir loft. Perched on the back of a chair. The congregation would not even look at me.

CLARA   *(beat)* And Maude?

CLARENCE   On the back of a chair, preparing to spring up towards the ceiling.

      She waits for him to continue.

It sounds silly, I know, but it was... frightening. No one would listen to me. There was the... the... danger that they would all turn *against* me.

CLARA   Clarence—

CLARENCE   But *she's* the one in the wrong! She renounced her faith—

CLARA   But don't you think—

CLARENCE   There's no argument, no standing up for her, *she abandoned her faith and her church and her family! She was wrong!*

      He wants the subject to be closed, but after
      a moment she continues.

CLARA   After I saw her there with her children and sister-in-law, with a whole new life, I...

CLARENCE   What?

CLARA   Well, on the way home, I couldn't help but think of Ruth.

CLARENCE   Ruth?

CLARA   In the Bible. "Thy people shall be my people, and thy God my God."

CLARENCE   I can't believe you have the gall to compare my sister to *Ruth*!

CLARA   Because she left her native land, left Moab and its gods, and went to Bethlehem with her mother-in-law. And because she did we believe Ruth to be a good and virtuous woman, yes? But what would all her virtues mean if she had gone the other way, not from the gods of Moab to the god of the Jews, but from our God to those others?

CLARENCE   Oh, Clara, now...

CLARA   Then it would be the story of a traitor, isn't that so?

CLARENCE   But she didn't. And that's the point.

CLARA   But *if* she had. What of her love and loyalty to her mother-in-law and her husband's memory then? Would they mean nothing?

CLARENCE   Don't be foolish.

CLARA   It's not foolish to me. Because what I think about, what upsets me is.... Does this mean that loyalty and love, are they nothing in themselves? Are they only virtues if they're aligned to a particular version of worship?

CLARENCE   I can't believe you'd even think this! You don't know what you're talking about, Clara, you cannot possibly understand—

CLARA   Why not?

CLARENCE   Because you're a mere...

CLARA   *(beat)* A woman? Is that it? I'm a mere woman. I see.

CLARENCE   *(beat)* Maybe you should go and fetch Roberta.

>   *He turns away.*

>   *A ways apart from them, a small choir begins to assemble (includes DORA and ROSS).*

CLARA   Yes. I'll leave you to your sermon then. *(beat)* When we were children, how much simpler our futures seemed.

>   *After she leaves, he turns in the direction of her leaving.*

CLARENCE   Clara?

>   *But she has gone.*

               (whispers) I have done nothing wrong!

>   *A moment, then he takes out his pocket watch. He looks at it as he speaks.*

               (tentatively) "Search me, O God, and know my heart: try me, and know my thoughts: And see if there be any wicked way in me, and..." *(He is cupping the watch in one hand; he begins to speak with authority.)* "Am I not grieved with those that rise up against thee? *(He begins to pound the watch with his other hand–three times.)* I count them mine enemies. I count them mine enemies. I count them mine..." *(He stops, hanging his head.)*

>   *A small church choir has assembled with their hymn books. They begin to sing as CLARENCE puts the watch back in his pocket. The light begins to fade on him.*

CHOIR   *Go labour on spend and be spent–*
               Thy joy to do the Father's will:
               It is the way the Master went;
               Should not the servant tread it still?

>   *Transition to next scene.*

Scene 2: 1899

North-eastern Nova Scotia. A sultry summer day. A country church.

Young DORA and ROSS are in the choir.

CHOIR *Men die in darkness at your side,*
Without a hope to cheer the tomb;
Take up the torch and wave it wide,
The torch that lights time's thickest gloom.

　　　　DORA's eyes never leave ROSS. Is he ignoring her?

Toil on, and in thy toil rejoice;
For toil comes rest: for exile, home;
Soon shalt thou hear the Bridegroom's voice,
The midnight peal, "Behold I come!" Amen.

　　　　DORA laughs suddenly.

ROSS (*sharply*) Dora!

　　　　The choir begins to disburse, walking leisurely–another
　　　　man and woman, two women walking together,
　　　　a lone woman–fanning out slowly across the stage.
　　　　ROSS alone has not moved. Is there a tension
　　　　between them? DORA goes to him.

DORA (*giggles*) I'm so wicked. Will I go to hell, do you think?

ROSS Don't be silly.

DORA Oh, Ross—

ROSS Only old fools like your father think that way anymore.

　　　　The members of the tiny choir now drift apart singly,
　　　　until all five of them are standing alone and facing
　　　　upstage. There is something dreamlike in their move-
　　　　ments. Faint thunder in the distance. DORA and
　　　　ROSS are both focused on something or someone
　　　　a short distance away that we cannot see.

DORA   It feels like rain. We should go and collect—

ROSS   They're just playing, they're fine.

DORA   But... (*She stops, uncertain.*)

ROSS   Dora, dear—

DORA   But if it rains...?

ROSS   He's not sugar, he won't melt.

DORA   But he could catch his death.

ROSS   Don't be so silly! You mustn't coddle him.

DORA   Look, they see us.

> *She waves. A beat, and then ROSS waves as well.*
> *YOUNG JAMIE comes to them, a young boy about*
> *five or six.*

YOUNG JAMIE   Mother, Dad!

> *As soon as YOUNG JAMIE arrives, both adults*
> *turn their attention to him. It is clear that they both*
> *dote on him. ROSS picks him up and tosses him in*
> *the air.*

DORA   Careful! Don't—

ROSS   He won't break. How's my little man?

DORA   Are you being a good boy?

> *ROSS sets YOUNG JAMIE down.*

YOUNG JAMIE   We found a robin's egg!

ROSS   (*teasing*) Was it red?

YOUNG JAMIE   No. Blue.

ROSS   A blue robin's egg? That's some rare, that's special!

YOUNG JAMIE   Silly.

DORA   Do you know why this is a special day?

YOUNG JAMIE   A birthday?

DORA   It's somebody's birthday, somewhere. But today is
              the *very* last day in the *very* last August of the *very* last
              summer of a *whole* century. After Christmas comes,
              in the winter, it will be a whole *new* century.

YOUNG JAMIE   That's a hundred?

ROSS   Yes, it's a hundred years.

YOUNG JAMIE   Like Sleeping Beauty.

DORA   That's right. She fell asleep for a hundred years. And
              do you know something?

YOUNG JAMIE   What?

DORA   When that prince woke her up, she was *almost* as
              happy to see him as we were the first time we saw
              you.

              YOUNG JAMIE turns to go.

              (*with an edge of fear*) Jamie, stop!

              YOUNG JAMIE stops and turns.

              Come back now, it's going to rain.

ROSS   Go on play with your cousin Mac, son, you'll be
              fine.

              YOUNG JAMIE looks from one parent to the other.

DORA   Ross.

ROSS   You don't need to pamper him so.

DORA   There's thunder in the air, I want to take him home.

ROSS   Let the poor boy be.

              Lightning in the distance.

DORA   Look, see. We should go. It's dangerous!

              Lights darken.

ROSS   (*exasperated*) Dangerous! Don't be such an old
              woman!

DORA	But it's going to storm!
ROSS	And what of it? We love a good storm, don't we, son?

ROSS takes YOUNG JAMIE's hand and they move away from her as the world turns very dark.

DORA   JAMIE!

YOUNG JAMIE and his father have joined the others standing about on the stage, a world of shadows. The air is dark and ominous.

Ross, bring him back!

Thunder. Lightning.

JAMIE! JAMIE!

Thunder, very loud and close. Blinding lightning. Then dark.

Jamie, where are you?

Darkness. The people fall to the ground.

(in the dark) JAMIE!

The thunder and lightning become gunfire that builds and fades.

Scene 3: 1917

Passchendaele, a wasteland of mud. Midnight. Sporadic shooting, cries for help.

JAMIE is lying on a slope, wounded, his clothes are encrusted with mud.

PAUL is not yet seen.

The scene gradually becomes slightly visible. There is the danger that JAMIE could slide into a shell hole filled with dank water. In the darkness around him, barely visible throughout the scene, lie the wounded

*and dead. The wounded cry out throughout the
scene.*

DORA   *(in the distance)* Jamie!

PAUL   *(loud whispers, calling)* Jamie?

DORA   *(growing fainter)* Jamie?

PAUL   Jamie?

JAMIE   Here.

PAUL   Jamie?

JAMIE   Paul? Over here.

VOICE 1   *(weak)* Help me! Help!

PAUL crawls to JAMIE.

JAMIE   Here! Paul?

PAUL   There you are.

JAMIE   Not going anywhere soon.

PAUL   I got so turned around. I was scared there I wouldn't
find...

VOICE 2   Here! Help! Mike?

JAMIE   Is anyone left?

PAUL   I don't know. Norm's dead, and Georgie and
Tommy, and I think I just saw Davy, but it's hard to
tell if that's who.... Most of his face.... Aw *Jesus.*

JAMIE   Lionel?

PAUL   No, he's gone.

VOICE 2   Mike? Mike?

GERMAN   Franz?

VOICE 2   Shut up, Fritz fucker!

GERMAN   *Verpiss dich!* [*Fuck off!*]

VOICE 1   Fuck you!

GERMAN	*Fick dich!* [*Fuck you!*]
VOICE 1	Fuck fuck fuck fuck...
	A moment.
JAMIE	I hate us all.
PAUL	Poor bastards.
JAMIE	When will anyone find them? They just sink and—
PAUL	Ssh.
JAMIE	Nothing's been real for weeks now. Not since Mac—
PAUL	Just hold on, dear, we'll get you out of here. Just hold on.
JAMIE	I can't, I just can't—
PAUL	I know. But you can.
JAMIE	And look—here—this corner of shit. All for this corner of...
PAUL	Maybe if we were just over on the ridge there, it would be...
JAMIE	Don't go off again!
VOICE 2	Mike? Mike?
JAMIE	*Please!*
PAUL	I won't now. Don't worry.
JAMIE	They'll try and make you—order you to.
PAUL	Ssh. Stop, just.... Lie still, I'm just going to have a look at where you...
	PAUL gently scrapes at the mud on JAMIE's chest, attempting to open his coat and see how badly he has been wounded.
JAMIE	Back home, the Tantramar Marsh—'f you bombed the shit out of that, end up with this?
PAUL	We're below sea level here though.

JAMIE	Right. *(beat)* We're at the bottom of the sea.
PAUL	I suppose.
JAMIE	The Sea of Shit.
	PAUL realizes the seriousness of the wound, but says nothing.
	I'm cold.
PAUL	*(beat)* Hippopotamus'd be more use to us here than those poor horses were.
JAMIE	Goddamn crime to do that... to those animals.
PAUL	You're right there.
VOICE 1	Help!
PAUL	Whole situation's waterlogged.
GERMAN	*Bitte!* [Please!]
PAUL	*(an attempt at a joke)* But the place sounds so pretty, you have to admit.
JAMIE	What?
PAUL	First time I heard tell of it I thought of a little place you'd come to walking through birch trees. With a little brook where you'd sit with your sweetie.
JAMIE	*(beat)* My mother—I was wee—took me in the woods—place there, pretty place—said, "This is where your father and I first thought of you."
PAUL	*(a joke)* Do you suppose that she meant that she and your father... did it? In the woods?
JAMIE	Who knows? *(beat)* She'll never recover 'f I don't come back.
PAUL	Ssh.
JAMIE	Serves me right.
PAUL	No.

JAMIE	Signed up to prove her I could. Why couldn't she leave Sarah and me alone? Thought I'd be back home quick as a wink and she wouldn't be able to touch me then. She'd see I'm all grown up and leave us be finally.
PAUL	Ssh...
JAMIE	They say how some men marry their mothers? Not me. No sir. Sarah's not like my mother—one bit. Hope to Christ she'll find someone else. Can't believe I'd say—but I screwed a girl in London—didn't think of her at all. No guilt—separate entirely. Sarah's—she's—what's that word...
PAUL	Just rest.
JAMIE	Word that...
PAUL	It'll be dawn before too long and we can get you out of here.
JAMIE	Pragmatic. Sarah. Yes.
PAUL	Shh.
	They are quiet. PAUL is holding onto JAMIE so that he won't slide down into the mire.
JAMIE	When we took that pillbox...
PAUL	Don't now, ssh.
JAMIE	But they squealed like pigs, didn't they? Just like pigs. Poor piggies. Like shooting pigs.
PAUL	Jamie, don't—
JAMIE	They had piggy wives—and piggy girlfriends and piggy mothers—and little piggy girls like my little piggy Helen—
PAUL	*Stop.*
JAMIE	*(beat)* I think I just shit my pants.
	PAUL starts to laugh, laughing or crying? It's hard to tell.

	What's so funny?
PAUL	The Empire doesn't get much more glorious than this, does it?

They both laugh.

JAMIE	I'm very frightened.
PAUL	Yes. Me too.
JAMIE	I'm glad you're here.
PAUL	Yes. Me too. I just wish here was somewhere else.
JAMIE	Baghdad.
PAUL	Yes, with Ali Baba's girls from the chorus.
JAMIE	There's something that's so...
PAUL	Yes?
JAMIE	I know you like I'll never know Sarah. Understand?
PAUL	I think so, yes.
JAMIE	Because nothing else is as big as this, is it? Nothing ever will be.
PAUL	No.
JAMIE	Please... something...
PAUL	Yes, dear?
JAMIE	Kiss me?

PAUL looks at JAMIE and then kisses him gently on the cheek.

No, idiot, not like my mother. But like—

And JAMIE pulls PAUL close and tight to him and they kiss long and passionately. JAMIE's arm holds him so tightly, then lets go and falls. PAUL pulls his head away.

PAUL	Oh, never, have I ever...

JAMIE doesn't move. PAUL sits up, not knowing what to do. After a moment he genuflects. Then sits. And sits. Thunder in the distance.

Lights fade to black.

Scene 4: 1939

Toronto, late on a Saturday night, a quiet street.

In the darkness, HELEN's voice singing a cappella, slowly and beautifully, the verse section of "Let's Fall in Love." DOLLY joins her on the last line.

The lights come up. HELEN, wearing a light coat over the spangly dress she wears on stage, walking home late at night with her friend DOLLY.

DOLLY   And are you?

HELEN   What?

DOLLY   Stalling? Falling?

HELEN   Bawling my eyes out, maybe. Oh... I don't... I wish, I *wish*...!

DOLLY   But Helen, don't you *love* him?

HELEN   I don't know! I think so maybe. He said it was an early birthday present—and I said, "Four *months* early"—I didn't think—*a ring*—that he'd propose so darn soon!

DOLLY   The part I hate is that you move away. Edmonton, gawd!

HELEN   And, oh Dolly, yesterday, my mother—who was *dead set* against this—started talking about moving there, too!

DOLLY   No.

HELEN   *Yes.* She only ever came to Toronto in the first place 'cause of her brother, you know, after the war. And to get as far away as she could from Crazy Grammy, of course, that too.

DOLLY   She Who Cries.

HELEN   She Who Cries constantly. The weepingest mother-in-law in Maritime history, Mom says. *(beat)* And it means I'd have to stop singing.

DOLLY   Why?

HELEN   He wants to have a family. Right away.

DOLLY   Don't you?

HELEN   I guess I do. I don't know. Not yet. I don't know. Oh *damn!*

DOLLY   But look, Helen—you don't *not* love him?

HELEN   Oh, I love him, I think. Yes, I know I think I do love Ivan, yes.

DOLLY   Well then.

HELEN   But he's not my friend. He's not a talker. I'll really miss you!

DOLLY   I'm a real good letter-writer. We'll keep in touch. *(beat)* It was a good show tonight, hey?

HELEN   Yeah, it was.

DOLLY   Wanna come by in the morning for coffee before we go to church?

HELEN   Sure. Thanks.

> *They walk a bit, then HELEN stops.*

But all those sisters of his out there. Four of them! Four! And his mother and father want him to marry a nice Ukrainian girl, have lots of nice Ukrainian babies. At least if we got married here you could be my maid of honour. It wouldn't seem so... I don't know. I'm just afraid I'm going to be so alone out there! And married from his parents' house! Why did I say yes to any of this?

DOLLY	Because he swept you off your feet.
HELEN	Falling in love is such damned foolish nonsense!
DOLLY	That last name of his *is* a doozy.
HELEN	Oh God, you should hear my mother on that! "You'll sound like a foreigner," she says, "Can't he change his name? Jack Benny on the radio, he used to be Benjamin Kubelsky." She read that in a magazine somewhere.
DOLLY	Jack Benny's *Ukrainian*?
HELEN	No, I think he's Jewish. Lots of those Hollywood people change their names so they won't sound all foreign and different.
DOLLY	Why d'you suppose?
HELEN	You should know—you changed *your* name.
DOLLY	Just my first name, 'cause my father named me after that poem in school. Do you have any idea how much I hate that rotten thing? "To Althea from Prison" —*gawd*.
HELEN	Althea's nice—very classy, I think.
DOLLY	It's a dumb name, and no name for a singer.
HELEN	But why'd you decide on Dolly?
DOLLY	After the Dolly Lama.
HELEN	Huh?
DOLLY	The Dolly Lama, over in Shangri-La. *(beat)* I'm kiddin'. I picked it out of the air. *Althea. Gawd.* I wanted something feminine. *Althea.* Everybody always called me Al, like I was one of the guys. "Hey, Al, how ya doin'?" Gawd. Would Ivan change his name for you do you think?
HELEN	No, 'course not.
DOLLY	Where'd that come from, d'ya s'pose— changin' your name for some guy's?

HELEN	Probably in the Bible somewhere. Somethin' about chattel or coveting thy neighbour's wife. Or his ass.
DOLLY	Speaking of which. Ivan's pretty sharp lookin. Are all the men in Ukrainia that handsome?
HELEN	It's the Ukraine, silly.
DOLLY	Where's it at, anyway?
HELEN	I don't know—the Caspian Sea or the Steppes of Russia or somewheres over there. But his grandfather came over here last century. His father was in the war. *(beat)* Know what I realized the other day? I'm more than a year older than my father was when he died. Isn't that...? *(shrugs)*
DOLLY	Mine goes on and on about that damn war without ever really saying anything. Drives us all to distraction.
HELEN	It's so long *ago*. Mom and Crazy Grammy are still blaming each other for the fact that my father enlisted in the first place. Each one says the other drove him to it.
DOLLY	That guy who came to see you and your mother, that Paul guy who knew your father...
HELEN	I kind of wish he hadn't come.
DOLLY	Why?
HELEN	'Cause I don't think much about my father, there's not much point, and to hear him talk about how much my father loved me even though he never laid eyes on me, well, it just made me feel guilty, kind of. He didn't mean to, but.... But, oh Dolly, *what am I going to do?* If I marry Ivan, my whole life will change! Moving some place I don't know, no old friends, and a family that's just so different. And my mother tellin' me not to marry "some *bohunk*." But what if she's right? Will I always be an outsider there? How will they treat me? I just...

DOLLY	And what happens if you don't?
HELEN	We could be old maids together.
DOLLY	Oh, doesn't that sound like fun.
HELEN	No, but we could get a job singing with a real fine band, the Casa Loma Orchestra maybe or something. Tommy Dorsey.
DOLLY	*(get real)* Tommy Dorsey.
HELEN	Well, why not? We're real good. And if we practise real hard, we could be that good. And sing all over the place and be on the radio and have more than one fancy dress to wear on stage, and.... Why does falling in love have to put a stop to all of that? Why do I feel like a whole important part of my life, of *me*, will be over?

> *They look at each other. A moment.*

Scene 5: The Darkening Landscape

> *JOANNE comes running past DOLLY. She is in tears, and RANDY is behind her. They are in Edmonton, August 1974, afternoon. HELEN and DOLLY are gone.*

RANDY	Wait up! Jo! *Joanne!*
JOANNE	Leave me!
RANDY	Come on!
JOANNE	*(blubbering)* I'm so stupid, I'm just so—
RANDY	You're overreacting.
JOANNE	*(hysterical) I am not!*
RANDY	Calm down.
JOANNE	He's a—just a—such a—*oinkoinkoink*— Pig!
RANDY	Now...

JOANNE	Why didn't he just call me a slut? 'S'what he was thinking.
RANDY	He was not, he—
JOANNE	Don't you know the meaning of *subtext*! He thinks I'm a slut!
RANDY	Whatta you care? He's an old prick.
JOANNE	Why wouldn't she tell me she was leaving Vancouver? *Why?*
RANDY	You can still go there.
JOANNE	But it won't be the same—it won't be— I'm such an idiot!
RANDY	You don't have to go there to live with her.
JOANNE	But that was the plan! That's what we talked about! Why wouldn't she say she was moving to Toronto?
RANDY	I don't know.
JOANNE	Why wouldn't she tell us that she was moving?
RANDY	Maybe she's just too busy?
JOANNE	Too busy for *me*? *Why*? The plan was for me to go out at the end of the summer. *(beat)* What if she *was* the one who wrote "Return to Sender" and sent it back? What if it was Debbi *herself*?
RANDY	Don't now, don't—
JOANNE	And I wrote her a really good letter. *(She has it with her.)* Because I miss her and...
RANDY	She's just going through something weird maybe.
JOANNE	But her father said—
RANDY	I told you it was a mistake to go there.
JOANNE	I just wanted her new address. I just—
RANDY	He's a prick!

JOANNE	"If Deborah has decided not to give *you* her address in Ontario, then I certainly can't *divulge* it."
RANDY	What a prick.
JOANNE	"*Divulge* it"? I thought we were friends. Remember when we heard that Joplin was dead? On the radio? We're still lookin' at each other with our mouths open when Deb walks through the door with that little bottle of Southern Comfort.
RANDY	Maybe we can't keep doing that grasshopper thing. Maybe we have to... *(isn't sure how to continue)*
JOANNE	Have to what? Join the Establishment?
RANDY	No, we don't have to join the—
JOANNE	Grow up? Is that what you mean?
RANDY	Well, no, I—
JOANNE	'Cause I didn't think it was about *growing up*. I thought it was about being *different*, having a whole different set of different values.
RANDY	I'm not saying we have to sell out!
JOANNE	Then what? *(beat)* But we were really close! From way back! Grade eight! And last summer, when she and I hitchhiked everywhere—that was so, so... *important*. How could she just— I don't get it. Like in Nova Scotia. We smoked pot on my relatives' graves for fuck sakes! Doesn't any of that mean anything to her anymore?
RANDY	*(beat)* Debbi's been distant ever since, since that thing with the baby.
JOANNE	"*That thing with the baby*"!?
RANDY	Ever since—
JOANNE	"*That thing with the baby*"! That thing with the baby was called an "abortion."
RANDY	I know, I just— I hate that word.

JOANNE	Not as much as I hate "That thing with the baby"! Jesus.
RANDY	I'm sorry. *(beat)* Do you know what would've happened if *she'd* gotten pregnant?
JOANNE	What do you mean?
RANDY	If Debbi'd gotten pregnant instead of you. What would've happened.
JOANNE	What?
RANDY	Well, Mr. Oinkoink'd probably be my father-in-law right now.
JOANNE	No.
RANDY	Yes. She told me. She would've wanted to get married.
JOANNE	When did she say this?
RANDY	The day before she left. When I was helping her move.
JOANNE	She would have had to marry you?
RANDY	No. She would have *wanted* to marry me.
JOANNE	Because of the Oinkoinks?
RANDY	Partly maybe. But mostly because of her. What she said was that's what she thought *we* should've done.
JOANNE	We should have gotten married? Had the baby?
	RANDY nods.
JOANNE	But she never said anything to me, she never—why didn't you tell me this then?
RANDY	I don't know, I... I didn't want to.
JOANNE	So she thinks— Oh bummer, oh God, this is so, so... *worse* than I thought!
RANDY	No. She's just really... really straight, I think.
JOANNE	Yeah, and *she* thinks I'm a slut! The person who I believed was my best friend, who understood me

like nobody else in my life *ever*, thinks *I am a slut*. (*beat*) Oh, this is, this is the *worst* week in the *history of the world!*

RANDY   It could be worse. It's not all that bad. Maybe.

JOANNE   Tell me one good thing that's happened.

RANDY   Well...

JOANNE   One Good Thing.

RANDY   (*beat*) It looks like they'll impeach Nixon.

JOANNE   *Impeach?* That little prick should be *impaled!*

> RANDY *goes to comfort her, but she rebuffs him. She sits on the ground, knees up, hiding her face. RANDY watches her. They remain visible as the scene continues.*
>
> CLAIRE *and* PETER *are looking at a pocket watch; it is late in the afternoon before their grand-mother's funeral. They are in the same landscape as* JOANNE *and* RANDY. *The light begins to fade very slowly as the scene progresses.*

PETER   I think *you* should have it.

CLAIRE   But it's a man's watch.

PETER   Yeah, but it's useless, it doesn't work.

CLAIRE   Gee thanks, bro.

PETER   No, I mean you should have it like for jewellery or an antique or...

CLAIRE   It's really old, but I wonder if it's worth anything. Grammy's grandmother sent it to her when she got married. Did you know that?

PETER   I never pay attention to that stuff.

CLAIRE   It belonged to her father, Grammy's grandmother's father, that is. That's what Mom says anyway.

PETER   So our great-great-grandfather?

CLAIRE   You missed a great, I think. Our great-great-*great*-grandfather. Three greats.

PETER   Whatever. *(reads)* "Clarence..." Jeez, why did that name ever go out of fashion? *(reads)* "Mark 3:35." What's that?

CLAIRE   The Book of Mark or the Gospel or whatever. I looked it up in Grammy's Bible. Something like, "Whoever does the will of God, is the same as my brother or sister." Like if you believe what I believe, you're like my family, I think is what it means.

PETER   Huh. So Clarence was our great-great-great-grampy?

CLAIRE   I think so.

PETER   Do we know anything about him?

CLAIRE   He owned a watch.

PETER   So you want it?

CLAIRE   I don't want to throw it out. *(sighs)* Oh, I *hate* funerals.

PETER   What funeral have you ever been to?

CLAIRE   Grampy's.

PETER   You weren't even five, you don't remember going.

CLAIRE   I do so. And I remember their fiftieth anniversary, too—the cake with all those candles. I sat on Grampy's lap. But what I mean is, I hate the idea of them. It means that Grammy is gone for sure.

PETER   But she was old and sick.

CLAIRE   I know. *(beat)* Maybe what I really hate is the idea of having to deal with Mom and Dad being in the same room.

PETER   Yeah but it won't be for long. Your dad won't hang around after.

CLAIRE   I know. He'll just like head out with what's-her-name.

PETER   Missy.

CLAIRE   I know her name. *(beat)* Probably what I hate the
            most is that I have a stupid father who has a stupid
            girlfriend named Missy. *(beat)* It scared me. Grammy
            dying, I mean. I wanted to pretend like it wouldn't
            happen.

PETER   Yeah, well, it did.

CLAIRE   *(beat)* Dylan brought Mom flowers.

            An awkward moment.

            He's not going to come, he told her. To the funeral.

PETER   *(beat)* Have you talked to him?

            She shakes her head.

CLAIRE   Not since his birthday.

PETER   Good. That stuff he said about Laurel's dad.

CLAIRE   He was just...

PETER   He was just *nothing.* When things like this happen,
            you really find out which side people are on, like
            who your friends are *really.* He's a piece of shit, and
            I hope to fuck we never see him again.

            He hands her the watch.

            This should be yours.

            He leaves. She stands, watching after him.

            *RANDY has moved closer to JOANNE. The light
            continues to fade.*

RANDY   Clap Woman?

JOANNE   What?

RANDY   Clap Woman. *(beat)* Will you marry me?

JOANNE   Will I *marry* you?

RANDY   Yeah. Not because we have to, or *had* to, I mean,
            before... but—

JOANNE	*Will I marry you.*
RANDY	But because we *want* to. Because I wanna be with you, wanna... love you.
JOANNE	Marry you. *(beat)* Jesus Christ, Randy, have you heard nothing I've ever said, *ever*? Marriage? *Jesus Christ!* No!

He sits beside her.

RANDY	I'll do whatever you want.
JOANNE	But mostly I know what I *don't* want!
RANDY	Do you want to be with me?
JOANNE	I can't imagine *not* being with you, Ran, but...
RANDY	So why not?
JOANNE	Marriage? Never. I look at my parents' wedding pictures—at that white dress of hers—it's like something from the fucking Middle Ages. I mean, all that's missing is a pack of virgins trailing behind her waving palm leaves and carrying sheaves of wheat! I don't want that. When I told her about the abortion, she said, "Now we won't tell your father. He's got a lot on his plate right now at the Lion's Club."
RANDY	She's just trying to protect you both.
JOANNE	Oh, I know, and they're probably happy together—good ole Ivan and Helen—but I don't want that—I don't want to live every day with all that *compromise.*

They look at each other.

YOUNG JAMIE moves quickly across the stage, running/playing/moving past CLAIRE, and past RANDY and JOANNE. ROSS and DORA walk slowly behind him, not speaking. YOUNG JAMIE has gone on ahead. He is gone. Early evening. 1899.

When she can no longer bear the silence, DORA speaks. ROSS will not look at her.

DORA	*(beat)* Have you never loved me?
	He sighs.
	Ross?
ROSS	Oh, Dora, don't.
DORA	But never?
ROSS	Why are you...? *(sighs)*
DORA	Please.
ROSS	*(beat)* Everything you say and do is an irritation to me.
DORA	*(beat)* Everything?
ROSS	Every bless-ed thing.
DORA	Always?
ROSS	*(beat)* If only I had not come home from Halifax that fall. If only I hadn't gone to church that Sunday. If only— *(He stops abruptly.)*
DORA	*(beat)* But then you would not have a son.
ROSS	I know.
DORA	*(beat)* And is he "an irritation" as well? Is he—
ROSS	Stop! That's foolish and you know it. He's the only reason for anything.
	She stops and stands, feeling utterly alone.
DORA	*(beat)* Then what's to be done?
ROSS	"To be done"? Nothing. There is nothing to be done.
	A pause.
DORA	But we must do something! We're not just our own two selves. We have a little boy.
ROSS	There's nothing.

DORA	*(beat)* We must do our level best to give him a happy home.
	He looks at her.
ROSS	A happy home.
DORA	Yes.
ROSS	Oh, Dora...
DORA	For his sake. We must pretend to have a happy home.
	He says nothing, and starts walking away.
	Ross? *(beat)* Ross?
ROSS	For the love of God, Dora, what could *you* possibly know about a *happy home!*
	He leaves and DORA is alone.
	MAUDE and CLARA are talking. August, 1872. There's an awkwardness, a formality, to their conversation. Twilight.
CLARA	Thank you for agreeing to meet me.
	MAUDE nods–a beat.
MAUDE	You've had another baby.
CLARA	Yes. Dora. Clarence wanted to name her after Grandmother.
MAUDE	A good old-fashioned name, I suppose.
CLARA	Yes. *(beat)* Well... *(uncertain)* It's Clarence... *(She falters, unsure how to begin.)*
MAUDE	Is he unwell?
CLARA	No, he's...
MAUDE	*(beat)* Does he want to see me?
CLARA	*(shaking her head)* He doesn't know I'm meeting you. That is, oh, Maudie, I would like to try to attempt a reconciliation between you two.

MAUDE	*(beat)* I see.
CLARA	All this weighs upon him, I believe, more than he even realizes. He seems to take no delight at all in the baby, in little Dora, he seems so alone.
MAUDE	He has his faith.
CLARA	Oh, but he seems so unsure at times, as if his faith were a, a torment to him.
MAUDE	Well, that's where we differ, he and I.
CLARA	I beg your pardon?
MAUDE	Faith. Because mine sustains me. My faith and *my* family both. My *own* family, my husband and our children. When I go to Mass, I thank God for the gifts he has given me.
CLARA	Good. That's good.
MAUDE	I used to fret about whether my brother was weak and couldn't stand up to a petty tyrant like Father, or if he *really* believed that his faith dictated my expulsion. I fretted and worried about it constantly, but really, it's of no consequence in the end for, either way, Clarence has no affections for me, save hatred and anger.
CLARA	I don't believe that. No.
MAUDE	Pah.
	An awkward moment, as if the two women were suspended in time.
CLARA	He is never without the watch you gave him.
MAUDE	Ha.
CLARA	It's true. It's with him always.
MAUDE	And wasn't that the finest little watch I could find in all of Pictou County. And smartly engraved as well. Because he was about to go off to divinity school.

CLARA	It's with him always; he dotes on it. *(beat)* I believe that God is too great to worry about whether we sing his praises in Latin or English.
MAUDE	Good.
CLARA	Or Hindoo for that matter.
MAUDE	I agree. *(beat)* But I'm not as big as that. I am as *petty* as my own flesh and blood.
CLARA	Maude?
MAUDE	You see, I don't give a *tinker's damn* for Clarence or my father or any of my brothers *anymore*. It's not very Christian of me, but that's the way it is.
CLARA	But—
MAUDE	They have expelled me, hurt me, and I have *no desire* to reconcile with any of them.
CLARA	*(beat)* You and I, when we were young, we were close.
MAUDE	Yes, well, we're grown-ups now.
CLARA	Oh, but won't you help me? Won't you, please? Not for Clarence or me or you, but for little Robbie and Dora, for my wee girls. I don't want them growing up in a house that's—
MAUDE	*(cuts her off)* And why should they be any concern of mine?
CLARA	I beg your pardon?
MAUDE	Does my brother care about *my* children? Does anyone from my father's house? No. And so the welfare of your children is of no concern to me whatsoever.
CLARA	But—
MAUDE	Understand this, you: I would like to hurt Clarence as much as he has hurt me. No, I would like to hurt him *more*!
CLARA	How can you be so cruel?

MAUDE   Because I'm a human being! *(beat)* I know my brother.
          I know why he carries that fool watch with him still.
          I can just see him taking it out a hundred times
          a day and feeling sorry for himself.

CLARA   No.

MAUDE   Yes! He needs to carry it around with him, to take it
          out and feel guilty and ashamed because he couldn't
          stand up to Father. And do you know why he needs
          to feel that? Because he thinks that his suffering, his
          own suffering, is *Faith*! He thinks that is what faith *is*.
          (beat) I only wish the damned thing were some sort
          of explosive device.

CLARA   What do you mean?

MAUDE   There he would be on a fine Sunday preaching, with
          all of that betrayal and suffering and guilt ticking
          away inside his pocket. And I could swing by that
          church of his like one of God's avenging angels,
          I could come by and pull a lever or throw a switch,
          and blast the whole pack of you to kingdom come!

          *A moment, then CLARA, horrified, turns and moves
          away from her. Another moment, then MAUDE
          puts her hand to her face.*

          (whispers) Oh, Father in heaven...

          She hides her head.

          *HELEN is standing in a slip holding her wedding
          dress, clutching it in front of her, like a paper doll's
          dress. She has been crying, and is whispering to her-
          self.*

          *The other characters are present but barely visible in
          the darkness surrounding her, as if she were alone in
          a windowless room. The dress glows like the moon in
          a black sky.*

HELEN   Silly stupid—

> *IVAN appears and stands looking at her. He looks handsome and uncomfortable in his dark suit and tie.*

(embarrassed) Ivan.

IVAN	*(beat)* Your mother sent me up.
HELEN	Oh. *(beat)* But isn't that bad luck?
IVAN	*(shrugs)* Not as bad as if we don't get married.

> *A long moment—what is to be done?*

HELEN	I thought you might be one of your sisters, again.
IVAN	No. I'm me.
HELEN	I feel so foolish.
IVAN	No.
HELEN	Yes. Foolish. I was worried I'd get cold feet, but...

> *They are both nervous, but tender with each other.*

Do you hate me?

IVAN	Hate you?

> *He shakes his head—"No, of course not"—but doesn't move towards her.*

HELEN	Mother's so exasperated with me, and she.... And your mother and father must think me crazy.
IVAN	No, not crazy.
HELEN	What then?
IVAN	*(beat)* I don't know, yet. But not crazy.
HELEN	And your sisters!
IVAN	Shh.... Don't think about them.
HELEN	*(beat)* What's everybody doing down there now?
IVAN	*(shrugs)* Making polite conversation.
HELEN	What are they talking about?

IVAN   The invasion of Poland.

HELEN   Oh God.

                A pause.

"*You* were born in wartime," Mom always said, as if it were all my fault. *(beat)* Being born, I mean, not the war. *(beat)* When she married my father, Crazy Grammy came to their wedding all dressed in black, head to toe, as if it were a funeral. And she cried through the whole thing because she was losing her son. *(beat)* The package she sent that came yesterday? With that silly old watch that doesn't work? There was a picture of them in it, Crazy Grammy and my father. A little boy in a little suit. I'd only ever seen his wedding picture before. He's standing on his hands; Grammy's holding his feet in the air and they look so happy.... I don't know why seeing a picture of my father as a little boy has upset me so. *(beat)* Until you proposed, all I wanted was to get married, as an end in itself, I mean. But...

IVAN   But it's not an end.

HELEN   No.

IVAN   It's a big, big thing.

                She nods. A very long pause.

                So...

HELEN   So.

IVAN   *(beat)* Are we going to get married?

                She shrugs and then she nods her head.

                (tentatively) Today?

                Another long moment.

Because, you know, if you wait much longer, you'll probably be *married* in wartime, too.

She smiles. Then she nods and gestures with the dress.

HELEN Can you help me with this silly thing?

He comes to her and awkwardly assists her getting dressed.

IVAN What do I...?

HELEN Can you help while I step into it?

IVAN helps hold the dress; she steadies herself on his shoulder and steps into it. She puts her arms in the sleeves. None of this is smooth.

IVAN I can get your mother.

HELEN Oh, please, no.

IVAN *(teasing)* Or my sisters.

HELEN Just you, Ivan, help me, only you.

They work silently, with only the occasional word–"There," "This?" "Oh," "Thank you." There seem to be a great many tiny buttons–on the sleeves, up the back–and he assists her with these. The light on them is lovely and soft, an island of warmth surrounded by dark.

IVAN Done?

HELEN Yes, I think so.

IVAN Good.

HELEN sighs.

HELEN I'm probably as crazy as my poor grammy.

IVAN Then your grampy must have been a lucky guy.

They look at each other, touch each other.

I am so happy.

She nods, they smile, they move, are just about to kiss, when–

> *JAMIE suddenly appears, isolated, apart from everyone in his own tight light that grows brighter and brighter. All others disappear.*

JAMIE   Kiss me, kisses, kissing—

Fucking unfair no goddamn fair—my *life*!

Never no more nothing! Growing old, home, blue sky, river, Sarah, breasts, pussy, cookies, kisses—

Helen—baby never now never—

But but—

(savouring the words) Kiss kisses yes—

Oh Paul, Paul, your mouth—keep me here and alive and forever and your tongue your warm, warm, warm—

> *Light on him brilliant, blinding, then snaps out.*

> *PETER moves slowly towards us in a tight light wearing Canadian Armed Forces desert camouflage. All the others are gone.*

PETER   When I saw him walking towards us, something about the look on his face, something about how fuckin' angry and—

Just how much he *hated* me. Like I was lower than shit, you know, or—

Just that look he gave. And so like determined or fierce or something. And I thought "Oh Jesus, Jesus that much fuckin' anger I'm gonna die, I'm gonna fuckin' die just from the fuckin' way he's lookin' at me."

This is all in like two seconds.

And I start to go like this *(as if starting to raise a rifle)*

And he blows up. Like— *(He spreads his arms quickly.)*

He fuckin' blows himself up. His head hits the road, like *thump*, and there's one leg left and the rest—

His hands indicate scattering.

Like some horror movie gross-out thing—

And my buddy, he says, like a joke, "At least we aren't in fuckin' Baghdad."

Blackout.

Scene 6: The Sunny Day

Lights slowly up on CLAIRE and DYLAN, Edmonton, 2008.

The light builds gradually throughout the scene as the other characters are revealed. At first, there is a growing awareness of them—they appear as shapes and outlines in the dark—and then we begin to see them clearly as they enter or are revealed individually or in small groups. A warm, lovely, summer day.

CLAIRE   Do you know what's weird to realize? That they're real young. Teenagers even some of them. And they, they're so ready to die. I don't believe in anything that much, that strongly. So things for them must be pretty desperate, like pretty hopeless, to make them get that way. When they ran the country, they banned music. Like what kind of people ban *music?*

DYLAN   After my cousin Lana found Jesus and got reborn, she told us we'd all go to hell if we kept going to dances.

CLAIRE   She's like a Baptist?

DYLAN   She's like a *Taliban* Baptist.

CLAIRE   Ha. Know something stupid? The name still sounds romantic to me, Taliban. Know what it means?

DYLAN   Someone who goes to heaven to screw virgins?

CLAIRE   No. It means like, a student, but more like a seeker.

DYLAN   *(beat)* Why did you want to see me?

CLAIRE   Because I miss you so much. And then my mother saw your mother at Safeway so I knew you were back. How was Calgary?

DYLAN   'S'okay.

CLAIRE   *(beat)* Do you have like a girlfriend or...

DYLAN   No. *(beat)* How's your family?

CLAIRE   My dad's got another new girlfriend. She's nice, I guess, but—oh, she uses "scrapbook" as a *verb*. *(beat)* And my mother—she joined this soldiers' mothers' group. Fuckin' Joanne, what an idiot. She's trying to get them to study the Koran. Can you believe it? They all think she's insane.

        A figure is becoming clearer in the dark behind them. Once he speaks, we realize that it's RANDY.

DYLAN   And Pete's dad?

CLAIRE   Randy's really fucked up about the whole Afghanistan thing. He and Mom are like hanging out more now and not arguing so much. So that's good. Randy ordered all this Afghan music, then went on eBay and bought himself a *rabab*.

DYLAN   Rabab?

RANDY   It's carved from mulberry wood.

CLAIRE   It's like an *oud*, you know, like a lute?

RANDY   You pluck the strings.

CLAIRE   It's pretty cool, actually.

RANDY   *(matter of fact)* There's no hope without music.

CLAIRE   My mother was crazy to not marry him.

DYLAN   Lucky for you she didn't.

CLAIRE   I guess. Whatever. He's so a nicer guy than my father.

RANDY   It's one of the few decent things we've accomplished in the last million years.

>   *CLARA, DORA, and YOUNG JAMIE emerge from the dark. The boy is walking on his hands, and his mother is holding his feet. Her mother is behind her.*

>   *In the distance, MAUDE can be seen watching these three; they are unaware of her.*

DYLAN   How's Pete?

CLAIRE   All right, I guess. He emails me like every day he can. I think he like *belongs*, I mean, he has good friends there and he fits in and... *(shrugs)*

DYLAN   He still hates me?

CLAIRE   He never wants to see you again, he says.

DYLAN   *(beat)* So where does that leave us?

CLAIRE   I don't know.

>   *They are uncertain as to how to continue. CLARA and DORA are watching YOUNG JAMIE, who is a little apart from them, trying to do a handstand.*

MAUDE   *(quietly, sadly)* I count them mine enemies.

>   *YOUNG JAMIE falls, harmlessly. They smile and watch. It is as if RANDY were becoming aware of the boy as well.*

>   *As CLAIRE begins to speak, JOANNE, HELEN, and IVAN are emerging.*

>   *[Different castings and role doublings may allow for other characters, CLARENCE, say, or ROSS, or MAC to appear as well. If this is the case, they should do so as simply as possible.]*

CLAIRE   Before Pete was born, Mom went on this big trip with Grammy and Gramps. Grammy wanted to go to Scotland to see where her people came from, like way back, and Grampy'd been over there in the war, in Holland, and there was this anniversary thing. So they all went, the three of them. When they were there, Mom told me, they decided to go and to see where Grammy's father had died.

YOUNG JAMIE is close to JOANNE, HELEN, and IVAN.

JOANNE   My grandfather.

CLARA   My grandson.

DORA   My Jamie.

YOUNG JAMIE goes to his mother. He tries to stand on his hands, and DORA holds his feet in the air.

CLAIRE   In World War I. At Passchendaele. He wasn't buried there, but he like disappeared in the mud and was never found. His name's on a plaque or a memorial or something. Mom ended up naming Pete after him.

JOANNE   Peter James.

IVAN   He was just a boy, your father.

HELEN   It's always boys in wartime.

And abruptly and magically, there he is, JAMIE, in his new uniform as we first saw him. He's walking on his hands. He passes his mother and his younger self, passes his daughter and her husband. PETER enters a short distance behind him, walking on his hands as well. The lights are now warm and bright, a perfect day.

CLAIRE   I'm scared shitless for Pete, and I want to support him, because he's my brother, but...

DYLAN   *(beat)* In Calgary, I worked with this guy, like our age, his family was from Pakistan, but he grew up here, and he said that his family was never religious much,

like growing up, but that now he *is*, he says he *has*
to be.

CLAIRE   Right.

> *As DYLAN speaks, we see everyone sitting and*
> *standing in beautiful, clear sunlight. JOANNE is*
> *now with RANDY, IVAN with HELEN, DORA*
> *with YOUNG JAMIE. CLARA and MAUDE,*
> *each of them are alone and isolated. JAMIE and*
> *PETER are alone as well, but near to each other.*

DYLAN   (*beat*) Remember how weird everything was after
9/11? That whole week? No planes flying, and beautiful sunny days. At first it didn't seem all that big
a thing, but everyone kept talking about how the
world was all different now. I came over to see you,
and your dad was there with your mom and grammy,
and Pete and Randy came over and we all watched
the church service thing from England. And when
they played the American anthem, your mom started
crying.

JOANNE   I can't believe I'm crying at the fucking American
anthem.

CLAIRE   That's right, and we couldn't tease her about it
because we all felt it.

DYLAN   And it started to make a kind of sense to me. I mean,
why it was a big thing. Everything was horrible, but
there was the sense that like except for a handful of
these stupid, crazy killers we were all on the same
side. The whole world.

CLAIRE   (*beat*) And then they blew it.

DYLAN   Yeah. Like really badly. Like *we* could have done
a better job running the world. You and me. (*beat*)
Then your grammy played old hymns and songs on
the piano after.

HELEN   Let's have a tune.

RANDY   Something we all know.

JOANNE   Something sweet.

PETER   Something you used to sing when we were little.

CLAIRE   Mom sold Grammy's piano. It seemed stupid to keep it, like none of us can play it or anything, but after she died, when the movers came, it was so sad! *(beat)* "You kids are so lucky," she used to say—

HELEN   I was born in wartime.

CLAIRE   I loved it when she played that old stuff and we sang along.

> *At this point, CLAIRE and DYLAN should be close together. Everyone behind them is standing and sitting in the bright sunlight.*

(sings) Let's fall in love,

CLAIRE &
HELEN   Why shouldn't we
             Fall in love,

HELEN/
JOANNE & CLAIRE   Now is the time for it
                      While we are young,

CLAIRE   Let's fall in love.

> *DYLAN kisses her.*

> *Lights fade on the people behind them, and then the lights fade on DYLAN and CLAIRE.*

> *The end.*

Afterword

An ideal period arrangement of Harold Arlen and Ted Koehler's "Let's Fall in Love" can be found on the album *Lovable and Sweet* by Annette Hanshaw, on the Living Era label.

The Gaelic lullabye "Ba Ba Mo Leanabh" can be found on two albums: Mackenzie and William Jackson's *Notes From A Hebridean Island* and Mary Jane Lamond's *Bho Thìr Nan Craobh [From the Land of the Trees]*.

O ba ba mo leanabh	[O, hush-a-bye, my little baby
Ba mo leanabh, ba	Hush, my little baby, hush,
O ba ba mo leanabh	O, hush-a-bye, my little baby
Nì mo leanabhs' an Ba Ba.	My own little baby will go to sleep.
Eudail mhòir a shluaigh an Dòmhain	Darling, the people of the Great World
Dhòirt iad d'fhuil an dé;	They split your blood yesterday;
!S chuir iad do cheann air stob daraich,	They put your head upon an oaken post,
Tacan beag bho do chré.	A little way from your corpse.
Dhìrich mi Bheinn Mhòr gun anal	I breathlessly climbed the Great Mountain
Dhìrich agus thearn.	I climbed and I descended.
Chuirinn falt mo chinn fo d'chasan	I would put the hair of my head under your feet
Agus craiconn mo dhà làimh.	And the skin of my two hands.]

The hymn "Go Labour On; Spend and Be Spent" was written by Horatius Bonar; the tune should be to William Boyd's "Pentecost."

photo by Michael Holly

Don Hannah is a playwright and novelist who lives in Toronto and Lunenburg County, Nova Scotia. He was the inaugural Lee Playwright-in-Residence at the University of Alberta where he wrote *While We're Young*. In 2008, he directed his play *There is a Land of Pure Delight* at Live Bait Theatre in New Brunswick. As a dramaturge, he has worked with playwrights from across the country, and for five years was on the faculty of the Banff Playwrights Colony. His books include *Shoreline*, a collection of his plays, and the novel, *Ragged Islands*, which received the Thomas H. Raddall Atlantic Fiction Prize.

DATE DUE	RETURNED